JetFighter II
The Official Strategy Guide

SECRETS OF THE GAMES SERIES

NOW AVAILABLE

COMPUTER GAME BOOKS

SimEarth: The Official Strategy Guide

Harpoon Battlebook

The Official Lucasfilm Games Air Combat Strategies Book

Sid Meier's Civilization, or Rome on 640K a Day

Wing Commander I and II: The Ultimate Strategy Guide

Chuck Yeager's Air Combat Handbook

Ultima: The Avatar Adventures

A-Train: The Official Strategy Guide

Global Conquest: The Official Strategy Guide (with disk)

Heaven & Earth: The Official Strategy Guide

PowerMonger: The Official Strategy Guide

Dynamix Great War Planes: The Ultimate Strategy Guide

Falcon 3: The Official Combat Strategy Book (with disk)

VIDEO GAME BOOKS

Nintendo Games Secrets, Volumes 1, 2, 3, and 4

Nintendo Game Boy Secrets, Volumes 1 and 2

Nintendo Games Secrets Greatest Tips

Sega Genesis Secrets, Volumes 1, 2, and 3

Sega Genesis Games Secrets Greatest Tips

Official Sega Genesis Power Tips Book (in full color!)

Super NES Games Secrets, Volumes 1, 2, and 3

Super Mario World Game Secrets

TurboGrafx–16 and TurboExpress Games Secrets, Volumes 1 and 2

The Legend of Zelda: A Link to the Past Game Secrets

How to Order:
Quantity discounts are available from the publisher, Prima Publishing, P.O. Box 1260BK, Rocklin, CA 95677; telephone (916) 786-0426. On your letterhead include information concerning the intended use of the books and the number of books you wish to purchase. Turn to the back of the book for more information.

JetFighter II
The Official Strategy Guide

Pete Bonanni

Prima Publishing
P.O. Box 1260BON
Rocklin, CA 95677
(916) 786-0426

Secrets of the Games Series Editor: Rusel DeMaria
Managing Editor: Roger Stewart
Production Editor: Laurie Stewart
Production: Marian Hartsough Associates
Technical Editor: Robert Bonanni
Copyeditor: Judith Abrahams
Illustrations: Ocean Quigley
Cover Design: Wong and Yeo
Cover Photo Courtesy of Barry Rokeach
Adaptation to Cover: The Dunlavey Studio
Indexer: Katherine Stimson

Prima Publishing
Rocklin, CA 95677-1260

Every effort has been made to supply complete and accurate information. However, neither the publisher nor the author assume any responsibility for its use, nor for any infringements of patents or other rights of third parties that would result.

Some 3D models used in this book were provided courtesy of Origin Systems. The F-16, MiG-21, and MiG-29 were built by Chris Douglas. The YF-22 was built by Danny Garrett.

Library of Congress Cataloging-in-Publication Data

Bonanni, Pete.
    JetFighter II ; the official strategy guide / Pete Bonanni.
        p.   cm.
    Includes index.
    ISBN 1-55958-187-5 : $18.95
    1. JetFighter II. 2. Computer war games. 3. Fighter plane combat—Computer simulation. 4. Flight simulators. I. Title. II. Title: Jet fighter II. III. Title: Jetfighter 2.
    U310.B663   1992
    358.4'148—dc20
                                                                91-42147
                                                                CIP

92 93 94 95 RRD 10 9 8 7 6 5 4 3 2
Printed in the United States of America

Contents

JetFighter II
The Official Strategy Guide

1 **Fundamentals**

Well, bless 'em all, bless 'em all,
The needle, the airspeed, the ball,
Bless all the instructors who taught me to fly,
Sent me to solo and left me to die;
If ever your engine should stall,
Well, you're due for one hell of a fall,
No lilies or violets for dead Fighter Pilots—
Cheer up, my lads, bless 'em all.
—from the fighter pilot song "Bless 'Em All"

It was a standard butterfly setup. We started the maneuver from line-abreast formation with a 1-mile separation, then turned away from each other in order to increase our displacement to get room for a head-on pass. At about 3 nautical miles between jets on diverging headings, we started a turn back into each other for a head-on pass. On this butterfly setup we briefed a "fights on" call at the pass. As I approached the target, my game plan flashed through my mind. The other F-16 was limited to 18 degrees Angle of Attack (AOA) on this fight, so I would have a distinct maneuvering advantage. The F-16 has a switch in the cockpit that you can use to limit the AOA the aircraft can reach (and thus limit the maneuverability). This switch is called the CAT switch, and is used to keep you out of trouble when you are flying with "dirty" configurations (carrying bombs, Maverick missiles, and other air-to-ground loads). On this mission the instructor was using the CAT switch to limit the maneuverability of the F-16 to simulate a MiG-23, which is less maneuverable. I would have felt confident facing most pilots at this point in the fight. Flying in CAT III is a big disadvantage. Unfortunately, I was fighting Skip. Skip was not "most pilots." In fact Skip was a highly experienced Fighter Weapons School instructor and the best F-16 pilot in the world—and since the F-16 is the most maneuverable operational aircraft in the world, he was the best one-on-one fighter pilot on the planet. Still, I was not too worried, since the poor sap would be stuck in CAT III. On this early Nevada morning I was going to eat Skip like a grape.

We passed head-on at corner velocity, left to left. My game plan was simple: put my lift vector on him and pull max Gs until he was out in front. As we flashed by each other head-on at 2000 feet per second, I yanked back on the side-stick controller and put the jet into a very painful 9-G left turn. No matter how many times I do it, I never get used to feeling that giant G elephant sitting on my body. Two seconds into the turn my relative body weight had increased to 1440 pounds and I strained against the G suit to keep my vision from

fading. The fight went "two-circle" (a term we will discuss in Chapter 3, the air-to-air Chapter), and on the next turn inbound as we passed, we were no longer head-on. I had gained about 90 degrees of turn on him. I continued in a left turn, pulling as hard as I could on the stick with the engine in full grunt (full afterburner). On the next pass Skip was out in front. I had him. I switched the radar into the Air Combat Maneuvering (ACM) mode and locked him up for a Sidewinder shot. Just as the radar locked on, Skip started a pull into the vertical. He pulled the jet 90 degrees nose high. I pulled up as fast as I could to follow him and keep the radar from breaking lock.

I was breathing heavy from all that maneuvering at high *G* as I followed Skip straight up into the cloudless Nevada sky. As we reached 90 degrees nose up, Skip continued to pull the nose of his Viper down toward the horizon as if he were doing a loop. I hadn't gotten a Sidewinder shot because as I followed his jet up I'd gotten jammed inside Rmin (minimum missile range). Inside Sidewinder range you use your gun. I called up the gun mode and kept pulling on the stick to follow Skip. As I started to pull my jet toward the far horizon from an inverted position, I noticed that the nose of the aircraft started to search a little from side to side. I didn't think anything of it and I kept pulling. Then it happened. The nose suddenly sliced down and the jet rolled violently into an upright position. I released the stick with my heart in my throat. The jet had "departed." In other words, the jet I was now riding in (not flying) had departed controlled flight and was completely out of control. Of course, right at the moment my pea-brain failed to register this fact. I thought to myself, "Airspeed, check your airspeed. I can't be out of control, I have plenty of smash [airspeed] on this jet." Glancing down at my airspeed indicator, I was surprised to see that it read 0. Zero airspeed—I was sitting in an F-16 and going at the same speed as a guy parked at the drive-through window at McDonald's. Little old ladies in tennis shoes out to get the morning paper had more forward speed on their bodies than I did at this instant in time. The AOA indicator was pegged at 32 degrees and the nose of the aircraft was oscillating slowly in pitch. After the initial departure, this position felt relatively comfortable, with the jet in a generally stable position at 1 *G*. Of course the realization that the high Nevada desert was rising up to pulverize me made this particular moment of my life far from comfortable. For what seemed liked minutes but was really only a few seconds, I just sat there riding a very expensive pile of aircraft parts toward the desert floor.

In the F-16, this position is called a *deep stall*. After an F-16 departs, it will enter a deep stall and just fall to the ground in an upright position. The flight control computers vote the pilot out of the command loop, and regular flight control inputs from the pilot are useless. This particular flight regime was not discovered in the early flight tests of the aircraft. In fact, the aircraft entered service with this condition completely unknown. It didn't take long, however, for operational pilots to fly the aircraft into deep stalls, which resulted in aircraft losses. The fix for the deep stall was to install a Manual Pitch Override (MPO) switch in the cockpit. With the MPO switch engaged, the flight control computers (which have voted the pilot out of the loop) are bypassed, allowing the pilot to control the horizontal tail. The horizontal tail is used primarily to control the aircraft in pitch, so with the MPO engaged, the pilot can rock the aircraft out of the deep stall with forward and backward force on the control stick.

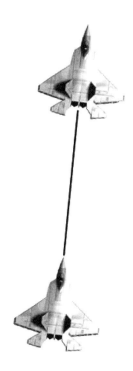

After coming to my senses, I did what every fighter pilot does in critical situations—executed the procedures I've been trained to perform. In this case the procedures for out-of-control are called BOLD FACE procedures and each pilot must memorize them and write them down at the start of each month. I now started to execute the F-16 BOLD FACE for Out-of-Control:

1. **Throttle: Mil if in AB.** In this case my engine was in full AB (afterburner), so I snapped the throttle to Mil (military thrust is the highest power setting short of AB).

2. **Controls: Release.** This is an easy one—you just let go of the stick. Since you were the bozo who flew the jet into this position, in many cases letting Newton's Laws take over will fix a faulty stick actuator problem. I let go of the aircraft side stick controller but it didn't help. I was definitely still hung up in a deep stall.

If inverted:

3. **Rudder: Opposite Turn Direction.** I wasn't inverted, thank God, so I skipped this step.

4. **MPO Switch: Engage and Hold.** I grabbed the MPO switch and held it forward in the Engage position.

5. **Stick: Cycle in Phase.** This is the critical part of bringing an F-16 out of a deep stall. When the jet enters a deep stall it will oscillate slightly in pitch. The trick of getting out of one of these stalls is to get in phase with the jet by cycling the stick.

It generally takes about 3 to 5 seconds for the F-16 to complete a cycle from nose up to nose down and back to nose up. As I started to cycle the controls, I started by pulling back on the stick as the nose was rising, and immediately noticed that the nose came way up past 30 degrees. As the F-16 started to oscillate down, I pushed forward on the stick and the pointed end of the jet immediately went straight down to almost 90 degrees. In fact, it caught me by surprise and I almost pushed the nose past 90 degrees. Luckily, I saw it in time and stopped it at 90. Going past 90 degrees on a deep stall recovery can put you into an inverted deep stall.

As I dove straight down, I noticed my airspeed was approaching 200 knots (nautical miles per hour). The book says that when you reach 200 knots you're out of the deep stall. I breathed a sigh of relief as I started to level off. Just then I heard Skip call, "Atoll." The whole time I'd been fighting to get out of the deep stall, Skip had been maneuvering for an Atoll shot (an *Atoll* is a Russian-built heat-seeking missile, similar to our Sidewinder). Before I could break to defend myself, Skip called a second Atoll, which ended the fight. I had entered the fight with a big advantage and ended up getting "killed" after flying the jet out of control. You might say I was having a bad day at the office (especially in light of the fact that I'd almost smashed my "office" to pieces on the surface of the high Nevada desert).

Well, I relearned a valuable lesson during this mission. You can't fight effectively unless you're aware at all times of your position in the jet's maneuvering envelope. This chapter will cover the basics of controlling your aircraft. This material is important because without knowing the basics, you can never master the more complicated tactical aspects of JetFighter combat. On the morning I deep-stalled that jet, I lost the fight because I forgot the fundamentals of aircraft control. Before we start to wax the bad guys, we'll discuss the basics in order to build a solid foundation for the tactical discussions that will come later in the book.

I will admit up front that my knowledge of aerodynamics is currently limited. This, despite the fact that I took a number of Aeronautical Engineering courses at the all-boy school I attended in Colorado (back when I thought that a Low Yo-Yo was a toy with a particularly long string). Since that time I have developed deep lines on my face in the course of a few too many wild nights and way too many close calls while strapped into various types of ejection seats. When I think of my knowledge of aero these days, the word "minuscule" comes to mind. I do know that when you pull back on the stick the houses get smaller and when you push forward on the stick they get bigger. Since that's about all I know and since I am currently flying about 10 fighter sorties a month, I don't think you need to know any more about aero than I do now. I will, however, risk giving both of us a migraine by going over a few very basic but important principles in the next few paragraphs.

Counterbalancing Forces on the Jet

Understanding the basic forces that act on the jet in flight will clear up the great mystery of why the pointed end goes through the air first. Figure 1-1 shows these forces and their directions in relation to the F-23.

Thrust pushes the jet through the sky, and is produced by an aircraft engine. In the case of a fighter, a jet engine essentially sucks air in through the intake, squeezes it in the compressor, mixes the air with fuel in the combustor, and ignites it, causing the air to blow out the back of the jet through the nozzle. On the way out the back end,

BASIC
AERODYNAMICS

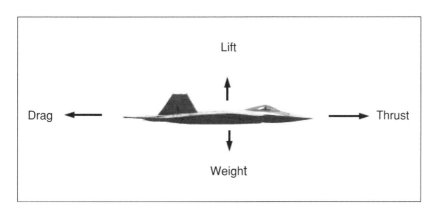

Figure 1-1. Forces acting on the jet

this high-velocity air spins turbine blades that power the compressor and the fan blades at the very front of the engine. The nozzle in the back of the engine closes down at higher throttle settings to create higher-velocity air (and more thrust). When the afterburner is engaged, fuel is literally sprayed into the aft end of the engine, just short of the nozzle, causing a controlled explosion that is directed out of the nozzle. The AB produces an enormous increase in thrust. During afterburner use, the nozzle opens because of the huge airflow (and the flame) coming out the back of the jet. The whole process of a jet engine can be summed up as: suck, squeeze, mix, ignite, and blow. Throttle position controls the amount of thrust that an engine produces by metering the fuel burned in the combustor. Throttle settings are usually measured in percentage points: 100 percent is the highest non-afterburning setting. This throttle position is referred to by fighter pilots as Mil. As you push the throttle up, you simply convert more jet fuel into noise and produce more thrust (and speed). You also burn more fuel.

Lift is a force produced by the aircraft wings and possibly by the body of the aircraft, and acts perpendicular to the aircraft's path, straight out from the top of the jet. A modern aircraft such as the F-23 uses a blended fuselage body to produce a great deal of lift. This saves aircraft weight by allowing the wings to be made smaller.

Drag acts in the opposite direction from thrust, and is created primarily in two ways. The first way is by basic aerodynamic shape. Pushing anything through air causes what is known as *form drag*. You can reduce form drag by having an aircraft with a smaller frontal cross section and by using a cleaner aerodynamic shape. A dart, for example, has a very clean aerodynamic shape and low form drag, while a cinderblock has a dirty, high-drag shape. The other type of drag is called *induced drag*. Induced drag is created whenever lift is generated. The explanation of why induced drag is produced by lift is beyond the scope of this discussion, but I think it has something to do with inverse tangents and imaginary numbers. If I had more time I would explain this phenomenon mathematically, but for now, since I don't have the time (and don't like to show off), just remember that as you turn the aircraft tightly you're commanding increased lift from the wings and thus are increasing the effect of induced drag. Induced drag is the dominant form of drag with the aircraft at slow speed, and form drag produces the most aircraft drag at high speed.

One final word on drag. You may wonder why a hard turn causes airspeed bleed-off in the JetFighter simulation. This reason this occurs is that under *G* (acceleration caused by turning the aircraft), the effective aircraft weight increases and lift must go up to counter the increase. With more lift comes more induced drag, so the airspeed bleeds off. To counter this you need more thrust. Unfortunately, aircraft thrust is always limited, which limits the *G* available and thus limits maneuverability. This is the reason modern fighters have thrust-to-weight ratios of 1/1 or greater. High thrust-to-weight ratios allow great maneuverability because they power an aircraft through the effects of induced drag. The effect of airspeed bleed-off during high-*G* turns is minimal in JetFighter when flying the F-23. This jet produces enough thrust to counter the effect of induced drag.

Weight is the simplest force to understand. Weight pulls the aircraft toward the center of the earth. Weight is a concept that even a fighter pilot can grasp.

JetFighter Maneuvers

Now that we're all up to speed on basic aero, it's time to discuss aircraft maneuvering in fighter-pilot terms. When it comes to maneuvering an aircraft, there are only three things you can do with a jet: *roll, turn,* and *accelerate/decelerate.* When you execute a roll in a fighter, you're positioning the wings, which in turn position your *lift vector* (there will be more on lift vector positioning later). Turning is nothing more than changing your flight path through the sky with the application of *G.* The more *G*s you command by pulling back on the stick, the faster you turn. Acceleration/deceleration is the change of aircraft speed and is caused by several factors. The forces affecting aircraft acceleration are thrust (throttle setting), drag, and aircraft nose position in relation to the earth. In the air-to-air chapter we will discuss maneuvering the jet in a one-on-one aerial fight. This type of maneuvering can be boiled down to simply positioning the *lift vector* of your jet in relation to another aircraft. For now, all you have to understand is the relationship of your lift vector position to the

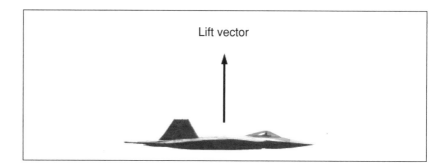

Figure 1-2. Aircraft lift vector

horizon with respect to *G*s. Figure 1-2 shows the aircraft lift vector coming straight up out of the top of the jet. This lift vector is produced by aircraft *G* and is controlled by the pilot. When the pilot pulls back on the control stick, he or she is commanding more *G* and a bigger lift vector. Since the aircraft moves in the direction of this vector, the more *G*, the faster the turn—or, in other words, the higher the turn rate.

Figure 1-3 shows a very important lift vector concept. In this figure you can see the number of *G*s (or the size of the lift vector) required at specific aircraft bank angles to maintain level flight. As you can see, at higher bank angles you need to pull more *G*s in order to stay level. If, for example, at 60 degrees of bank you were to pull only 1 *G* (instead of 2 *G*s, as in the chart), the aircraft would descend. If you pulled more than 2 *G*s, then the aircraft would climb.

Figure 1-3. Relationship between *G*s and bank angle for level flight

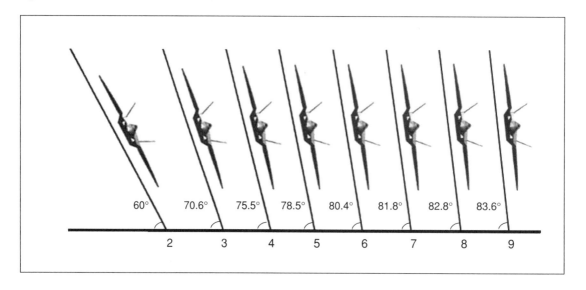

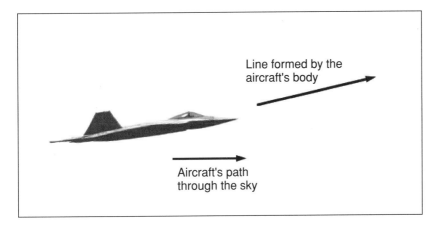

Figure 1-4. Aircraft AOA

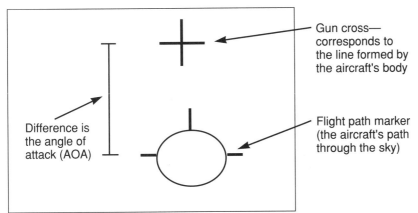

Figure 1-5. Gun cross and flight path marker showing AOA

What Happens When You Stall

It is hard to win an air-to-air fight in a jet that is stalled, so we'd better have a quick discussion of what makes an aircraft stall. *Stalls* are defined as the reduction in aircraft lift caused by an aircraft exceeding its critical *Angle of Attack (AOA)*. To understand stalls you must first understand AOA. AOA is the angle formed by the body of the aircraft and its flight path through the sky. Figure 1-4 shows AOA. In JetFighter the body of the aircraft, also known as the fuselage reference line, is represented in the JetFighter HUD by a cross, as shown in Figure 1-5. The difference between that cross and the flight path marker is the AOA. In JetFighter your AOA can also be read directly by calling up the CLS/ILS page on the MMD (left cockpit display). We will discuss cockpit controls and displays in the next section of this chapter.

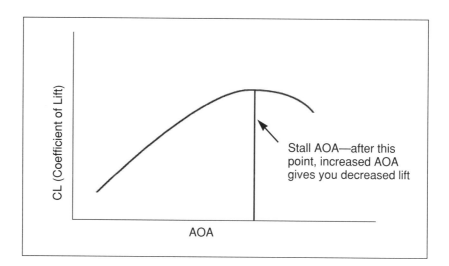

Figure 1-6. Stall AOA shown on a lift versus AOA graph

AOA is related to lift because as AOA goes up, so does lift. As an aircraft slows down, the pilot must raise the AOA to stay at a given altitude. The reason for this is that the total lift produced must be equal to the weight in order to maintain level flight. Lift is directly proportional to AOA and airspeed. What this means is that as you slow down, you will lose lift if you do not raise the AOA of the aircraft. With the increase in AOA, lift will also increase until the critical AOA of the aircraft is reached. At this point lift will stop increasing and will actually level off or decrease. This is called the stall AOA, and is depicted in Figure 1-6. As you increase AOA on the horizontal axis of the graph, the coefficient of lift on the vertical axis goes up. (For our discussion, think of the coefficient of lift as just lift). As AOA increases past the stall point, lift decreases.

The Different Kinds of Stalls

There are two types of stalls: stalls that occur at less than 1 *G* flight and stalls that occur at more than 1 *G*. Aircraft stalls that occur at less than 1 *G* flight are entered when the aircraft slows down and the pilot increases the angle of attack to maintain level flight. When the stall AOA is reached, the aircraft stalls. Stalls like these are easy to recognize because the aircraft will be flying slower than a known stall speed. This stall speed is equal to a specific AOA limit, which is reached in 1 *G* flight at a specific airspeed. This type of stall can occur in the landing pattern when a pilot fails to monitor aircraft speed and inadvertently flies too slowly.

Stalls that occur when the aircraft is loaded (flying at more than 1 *G*) are called *accelerated stalls*. These types of stalls are much more difficult to avoid, because they can occur at any airspeed. Remember that stalls occur when an aircraft exceeds its critical AOA. Airspeed can be translated directly into AOA (for a given aircraft weight) during 1 *G* flight. As *G*s increase, however, a combination of airspeed and *G*s will determine AOA. *Airspeed alone will not.* When you turn an aircraft at more than 1 *G*, you create two related effects that can produce an accelerated stall. The first is that at higher *G* you increase the size of your lift vector (you're producing more lift). Remember from our drag discussion that as you increase lift, you also increase induced drag. This increase in drag will cause your aircraft to slow down if it is not countered by an increase in thrust. The second effect is that any time you command high *G*, you raise the AOA and get closer to a stall. When you enter a high-*G* turn your AOA goes up immediately with the increase in *G*s; as you slow down it goes even higher, placing you closer to the stall AOA.

When you stall in JetFighter, remember that you have exceeded the critical AOA for the jet and must reduce the AOA by pushing forward on the stick. Also keep in mind that *a stall can occur at any airspeed if you are at high G.*

THE JETFIGHTER SIMULATION

The JetFighter simulation is very easy to get around in and most of the functions of the system are intuitive. Just in case anybody is fuzzy on what all those screens do, we will briefly discuss how to get into JetFighter and select the various options.

There are two basic menu paths in JetFighter. The first is the Main menu. This is the first menu that comes up when you enter the simulation. It provides the pilot with the primary means of selecting mission options. The second primary menu path is the InFlight menu. Any time you're in the cockpit of a jet, you can call up the InFlight menu to perform a variety of functions, including going back to the Main menu. The next section will cover both of these menu systems (including some shortcuts).

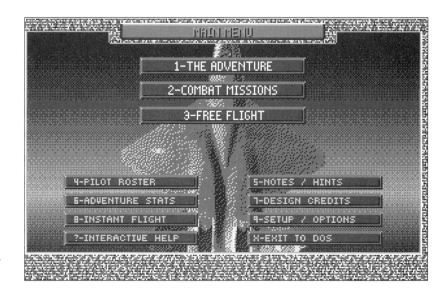

Figure 1-7. JetFighter main menu

The Main Menu

The Main menu is shown in Figure 1-7. It allows the pilot to perform the functions described below.

1—The Adventure

This option places you in a scenario-driven war game. In the Adventure, a pilot selects and executes missions in order to win a war. Records of performance are kept and the enemy also flies missions against your forces. The ultimate goal of JetFighter is to enter the Adventure and defeat the enemy.

Figure 1-8 shows a typical screen that comes up after you enter the Adventure. Once in the Adventure, you can highlight a mission by using a mouse or by pressing one of the number keys across the top of the keyboard or on the numeric keypad.

Pressing Enter places you in the cockpit for a selected mission.

Pressing Esc returns you to the Main menu.

2—Combat Missions

This option allow the pilot to fly independent combat missions. Each mission is an end in itself, and the record of the mission is erased after you review it. This option allows you to practice various combat skills without affecting the Adventure.

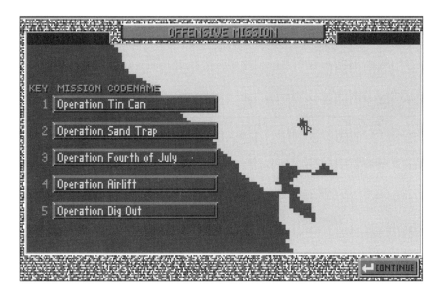

Figure 1-8. Typical adventure mission select page

Once you enter the Combat Missions page, you can select a mission using the number keys.

Pressing Pg Up and Pg Dn allows you to scroll through a very long list of available missions.

Pressing Enter starts the mission sequence.

Pressing Esc returns you to the Main menu.

Once you have started a mission sequence, you can select a particular aircraft with the A key and a weapons load with the W key.

After you select an aircraft and a weapons load, pressing Enter will place you in the cockpit for the mission.

3—Free Flight

This mode is used for training a pilot in aircraft handling, takeoffs, landings, and basic air-to-air combat. After you select this mode, a menu appears listing the following options:

Aircraft—pick your aircraft type

Bandits—choose the number of bandits (from 0 to 3)

Time of Day—use the arrow keys or the + and − to set the time

Take Off from—selects an airport or the carrier

Land at—selects an airport or the carrier for practice landings

Restart Session—restarts the Free Flight option

Resume Flight—puts you back in flight

4—Pilot Roster

This option allows you to add pilots to be used during the Adventure.

5—Notes/Hints

This option contains information on installing and running JetFighter. You can scroll through the information with Pg Dn and Pg Up.

6—Adventure Stats

You can use this option to review an individual pilot's performance.

7—Design Credits

This mode displays the names of the simulation's creators.

8—Instant Flight

This mode places you in the cockpit of a jet in flight at a randomly selected time of day.

9—Setup/Options

This mode takes you through the JetFighter setup pages and allows you to select a variety of simulation parameters and controls.

?—Interactive Help

This is a powerful option. It can explain various features of the simulation to a new pilot. After pressing ? to enter this mode, the pilot selects an area that he wants explained, and the simulation goes through a brief tutorial.

x—Exit to DOS

This option dumps you out of the simulation.

Figure 1-9. Options that appear after pressing the [Esc] key

The InFlight Menu

The InFlight menu provides the pilot instant access to JetFighter II simulation controls. Figure 1-9 shows the options that are displayed across the top of your computer monitor when you press [Esc] while in the cockpit. The InFlight menus are very important because they provide a way of quickly changing the simulation parameters without exiting from the cockpit.

Info

Selecting this option brings up the following list of simulation controls:

Display/Sound Options

Joystick Setting

Keyboard Controls

Design Credits

Resume Play

Exit to Main menu

Exit to DOS

For the most part, these options are similar to the ones on the Main menu, which we discussed earlier. The exceptions are the Joystick Setting option and the Keyboard Controls option.

Instead of selecting the Joystick Setting option from the menu, you can get to it more quickly by simply pressing $\boxed{J}$ after entering the InFlight menu.

The Keyboard Controls option gives the pilot "on-the-fly" access to the functions of all the applicable keyboard controls.

Free Flight

This is the same as the Free Flight option on the Main menu that we discussed earlier.

Missions

This option allows the pilot to quickly move around through the JetFighter mission choices.

CONTROLLING THE VIEW IN JETFIGHTER II

JetFighter allows the pilot to bring a variety of windows into the simulation. JetFighter initially comes up with a view from the cockpit, but the pilot can change to other internal cockpit views, or external views, and can even view the simulation from a control tower or from the nose of a missile or bomb.

Internal Views

The following is a list of internal view keys and their functions. You'll notice that all of them are on the numeric keypad.

KEY		ACTION
Numeric Keypad	$\boxed{-}$	Toggles between internal and external views
Numeric Keypad	$\boxed{7}$	Pan left
Numeric Keypad	$\boxed{9}$	Pan right
Numeric Keypad	$\boxed{1}$	Rear view
Numeric Keypad	$\boxed{3}$	Look up
Numeric Keypad	$\boxed{.}$	Look down
Numeric Keypad	$\boxed{5}$	Look forward

External Views

Again, all of the external view control keys are on the numeric keypad.

KEY		ACTION
Numeric Keypad	[−]	Toggles between internal and external views
Numeric Keypad	[7]	Swing left
Numeric Keypad	[9]	Swing right
Numeric Keypad	[3]	Swing up
Numeric Keypad	[.]	Swing down
Numeric Keypad	[1]	View from behind
Numeric Keypad	[5]	View from above

Preset External View

Another way to arrive at a specific external view is to just call it up by pressing [Shift] and the number of the view on the numeric keypad. This is the easiest way in most cases. (Note: Use only the numeric keypad, *not* the number keys at the top of the keyboard.)

KEY		ACTION
Shift	[1]	Aft and left of the aircraft
Shift	[2]	Dead 6 o'clock from the aircraft
Shift	[3]	Aft and right of the aircraft
Shift	[4]	Left of the aircraft
Shift	[5]	View from above the aircraft
Shift	[6]	Right of the aircraft
Shift	[7]	Looking aft from in front and to the left of the aircraft
Shift	[8]	Directly at 12 o'clock on the aircraft looking aft
Shift	[9]	Looking aft from in front and to the right of the aircraft

Other View Controls

The following are other view controls and the ways to activate them:

Control tower view—press [✱] above the numeric keypad.

Recording a specific view for later playback—press [Shift]-[Ctrl] and a number key. The simulation will record this view and replay it when you press [Shift] and a number key. This recorded view will be seen instead of the normal preset view.

Magnifying a view—all views can be magnified using the [<] and [>] keys.

Map view—press [M]. This map gives you a downloaded intelligence picture provided by the AWACS (Airborne Warning and Control System). You can also magnify the map view.

JETFIGHTER CONTROLS AND DISPLAYS

JetFighter provides the pilot with the option of flying several different aircraft. The aerodynamic models, cockpit displays, and available weapons change as you select the various aircraft, but the joystick and keyboard controls remain the same.

JetFighter Cockpit Displays

There are two JetFighter cockpits, the F-23 and the F-14/16/18. The F-23 cockpit layout is used by the other aircraft in the simulation (the F-14, F-16, and F-18). Figure 1-10 shows the F-23 cockpit with the different displays labeled. The most prominent feature of the F-23 cockpit is the three large CRTs that dominate the center section of the instrument panel. The screens that are available to the pilot on each of these CRTs are depicted in Figure 1-11. We will discuss the information presented to the pilot on the CRTs later in more detail.

Figure 1-12 on page 22, shows the cockpit of the F-14/16/18. You will notice that the information format presented in this cockpit is virtually identical to the one used in the F-23 cockpit.

JetFighter Controls

There are a few JetFighter controls that are worth highlighting before we start to discuss the flight controls and throttle. These are the speedbrakes, the landing gear, the arresting hook, and the wheel brakes.

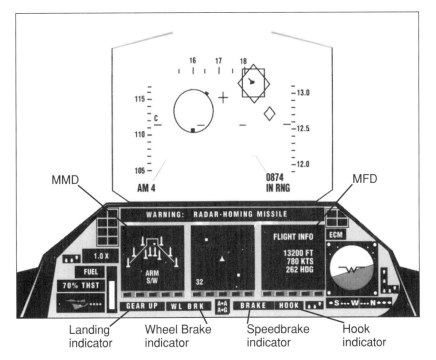

Figure 1-10. F-23 cockpit displays

MMD

MFD

Landing indicator

Wheel Brake indicator

Speedbrake indicator

Hook indicator

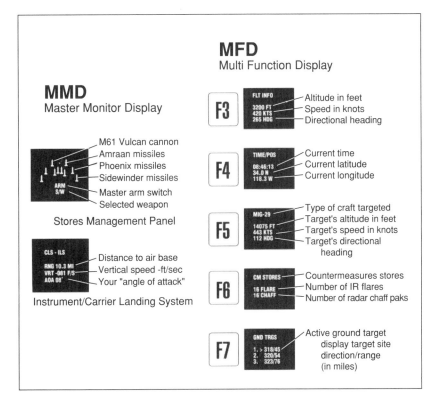

MFD
Multi Function Display

MMD
Master Monitor Display

M61 Vulcan cannon
Amraan missiles
Phoenix missiles
Sidewinder missiles
Master arm switch
Selected weapon

Stores Management Panel

CLS - ILS
RNG 10.3 MI — Distance to air base
VRT -081 F/S — Vertical speed -ft/sec
AOA 08° — Your "angle of attack"

Instrument/Carrier Landing System

F3
FLT INFO
3200 FT — Altitude in feet
420 KTS — Speed in knots
265 HDG — Directional heading

F4
TIME/POS
08:46:13 — Current time
34.0 N — Current latitude
118.3 W — Current longitude

F5
MIG-29 — Type of craft targeted
14075 FT — Target's altitude in feet
443 KTS — Target's speed in knots
112 HDG — Target's directional heading

F6
CM STORES — Countermeasures stores
16 FLARE — Number of IR flares
16 CHAFF — Number of radar chaff paks

F7
GND TRGS
1. > 318/45 — Active ground target display target site direction/range (in miles)
2. 320/54
3. 323/76

Figure 1-11. F-23 CRT display options

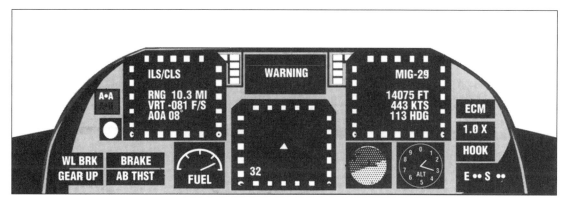

Figure 1-12. F-14/16/18 cockpit displays (showing different information than Figure 1-10)

Speedbrakes

The aircraft speedbrakes are applied by pressing (Backspace). The speedbrakes will be fully deployed when this key is pressed the first time, and retracted when it is pressed the second time. Speedbrakes increase the jet's form drag and are used to slow the aircraft down. Figure 1-10 shows the Speedbrake indicator. In both cockpits the BRAKE display will illuminate to indicate that the speedbrakes have been deployed.

Landing Gear

The Landing indicator is shown in Figure 1-10. This display shows either GEAR UP or GEAR DN to let the pilot know the position of the gear. Pressing (G) raises and lowers the landing gear. To a fighter pilot, raising and lowering the gear are second nature, but it can bite you if you're not careful. One of my best friends, who is highly experienced, landed a fighter gear-up.

Arresting Hook

The arresting hook is deployed by pressing (A). When the HOOK display, shown in Figure 1-10, is illuminated, the hook is deployed. Before landing on the carrier you must put the hook down.

Wheel Brakes

Wheel brakes are applied or released by pressing (B). When you enter the aircraft the brakes will be set and must be released for takeoff. When you're landing on a runway, the brakes must be applied to stop the aircraft. Brake status can be monitored in the cockpit by referencing the display shown in Figure 1-10.

Flight Controls

The pilot controls the aircraft through movement of the flight controls. In JetFighter you can move the controls on the aircraft either with a joystick, or by using the keyboard. (JetFighter very wisely does not feature a mouse-driven flight control system.) We will now discuss aircraft movements and the corresponding JetFighter controls that cause these movements.

Roll

Roll is movement of an aircraft around its *longitudinal*, or roll, axis. The roll axis is shown in Figure 1-13. In conventional aircraft, roll is

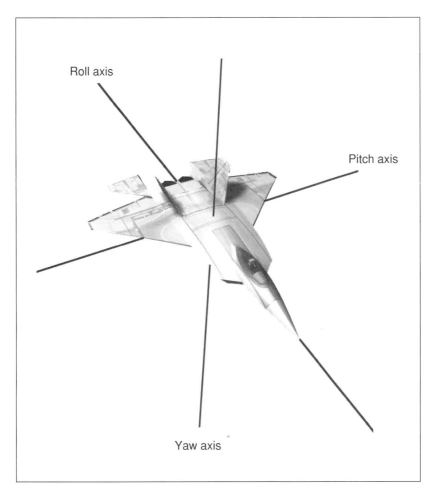

Figure 1-13. Roll, pitch, and yaw axis

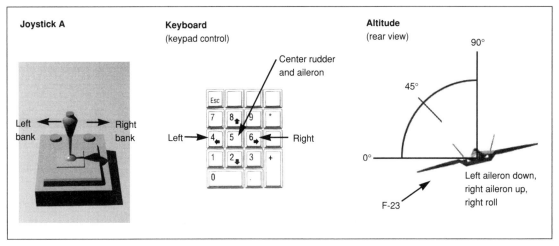

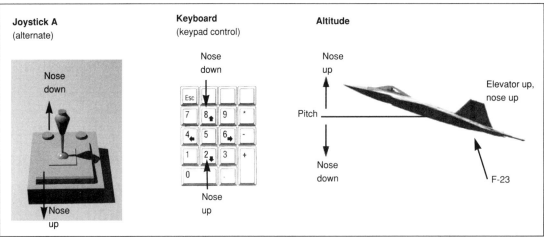

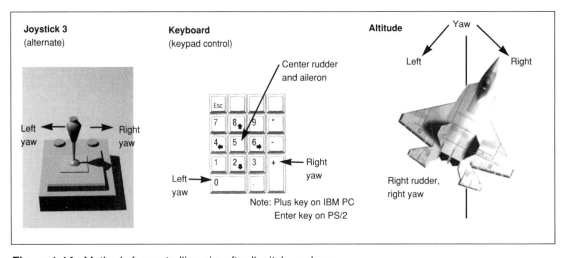

Figure 1-14. Methods for controlling aircraft roll, pitch, and yaw

controlled by an aircraft's ailerons, located outboard on the wings. These devices deflect up or down to either lower or raise the wing. Not all aircraft use precisely the same techniques for controlling roll. The F-16, for example, uses devices that are called *flaperons*. These devices act like a combination of ailerons and flaps. The specific control device is not important. What is important is that you know how to roll the aircraft using the appropriate JetFighter control mechanism. Figure 1-14 shows the methods used in JetFighter for controlling roll.

Pitch

Pitch is movement of the aircraft around the *lateral*, or pitch, axis. The pitch axis is also depicted in Figure 1-13. Pitch is controlled by the movement of the horizontal tail, or stab. Figure 1-14 shows the methods of controlling pitch in the simulation.

Yaw

Yaw is movement of the aircraft around the *vertical*, or yaw, axis. The yaw axis is shown in Figure 1-13. The aircraft rudder, located on the vertical tail, is used to control yaw. Figure 1-14 shows how to control yaw in JetFighter.

The Throttle

The pilot controls the aircraft thrust with the throttle. In JetFighter you can move the throttle in several ways, depending on how your PC is configured. Throttle control is accomplished with the keyboard.

The JetFighter simulation uses an innovative approach to keyboard control of the throttle, which is a very big help to the pilot but can also get you into trouble. The *number keys on the top of your keyboard* set the engine to specific thrust settings. For example, the [1] key sets engine at 10 percent of the maximum nonafterburning thrust; the [2] key, at 20 percent.

The [1] through [9] keys set specific throttle settings corresponding to each number times 10.

The [0] key puts the engine at 100 percent the first time you push it. The second time you press [0], the engine goes into Afterburner.

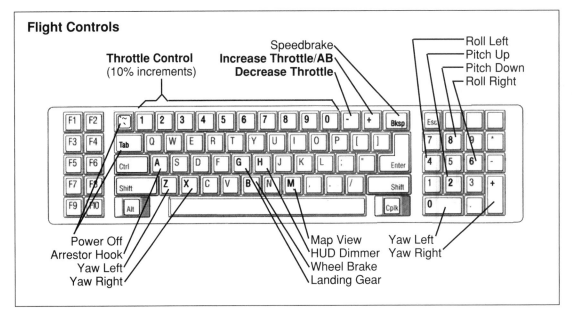

Figure 1-15. Keyboard throttle controls

Another way to control the throttle in JetFighter is to press ⊕ and ⊖. These keys advance and retard the throttle 1 percent at a time if pressed and released. If held down, they will continuously advance or retard the throttle. Figure 1-15 shows the keyboard layout, indicating the keys that control the throttle.

The position of the throttle can be monitored by looking at the RPM gauge, shown in Figures 1-10 and 1-12. As we have discussed, JetFighter features two basic cockpit layouts. In both the F-23 and the F-14/16/18 cockpits the throttle position can be monitored by reading a digital display. A reading of 100 percent is the maximum nonafterburning thrust, which is called Mil, or Military power. When the afterburner is selected in either cockpit, you'll see the letters "AB" instead of the digital RPM readout.

JetFighter HUD

The HUD, or Heads Up display, provides the pilot with critical information for routine flying and for combat missions. In JetFighter II the HUD is very simple and easy to use. Figure 1-16 shows the ILS (Instrument Landing System) display in the HUD with all the information labeled. The combat modes of the HUD will be discussed in detail in later chapters.

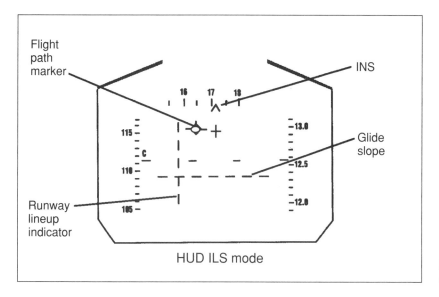

HUD ILS mode

Figure 1-16.
JetFighter ILS display

The time has come to strap yourself into this beast and get some air between your butt and the old *terra firma*. On this mission we will perform the following maneuvers:

- Takeoff
- 1 *G* Stalls
- Accelerated Stalls
- Navigation
- Landings

The objective of this sortie is to get you familiar with the jet in preparation for combat.

JETFIGHTER TRAINING SORTIE

Setting Time of Day

To get started on this mission:

1. Select Free Flight from the Main menu (shown in Figure 1-17).
2. Select Time of Day by pressing T.

We will fly this mission at 1300 (pronounced "thirteen hundred"), so we must set the time. This is military time—1300 is equivalent to 1 PM civilian time.

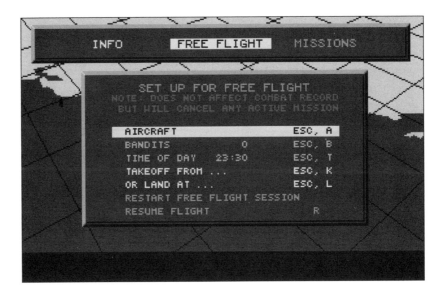

Figure 1-17. Free
flight menu

3. To get there from here you must alternately press the → and ← keys to select the hours or minutes setting to be changed. After you select hours or minutes, you can change the time with the + and − keys.

4. After setting the time of day at 1300, exit this mode by pressing Esc.

5. Next, go down to the Takeoff From option by pressing K and select Los Angeles International by pressing Enter.

You will be transported to the cockpit of the F-23 on the runway at Los Angeles.

   Before we get started, let's discuss some other useful simulation controls. A very big aid when you are first learning JetFighter is the P key. The P key pauses the simulation. Use it liberally during this training flight to check your cockpit controls and the HUD. (Unfortunately, when you pause the simulation, a big Pause screen blocks out a large portion of your view.) Another useful feature of the Free Flight mode is the Restart function. If at any time during a mission in the Free Flight mode you need to restart the simulation, press Esc, enter Free Flight, and then select the Restart Free Flight option.

Takeoff

You are now in the cockpit and ready for takeoff. Take a minute to find the HUD airspeed scale and the HUD flight path marker. Once you've found those displays, you're ready for takeoff.

Use the following steps for takeoff:

1. Press $\boxed{0}$ to run the power up to 100 percent.

2. As the engine passes 80 percent, release the wheel brakes by pressing $\boxed{B}$.

3. Roll straight down the runway. When you reach 150 knots, smoothly rotate the jet by pulling the flight path marker above the horizon.

4. As the jet accelerates past 200 knots, as shown in Figure 1-18, raise the gear with the $\boxed{G}$ key and keep climbing until you reach 5000 feet.

5. Press $\boxed{5}$ to retard the throttle to 50 percent, and level off the jet by pushing the flight path marker down to the horizon.

With the flight path marker on the horizon, the aircraft will stay level. You should now be close to 6000 feet, flying straight and level. Don't worry if you're not at this altitude. The point here is to note the relationship of the flight path marker to level flight. The only way to fly level is to put the flight path marker on the horizon.

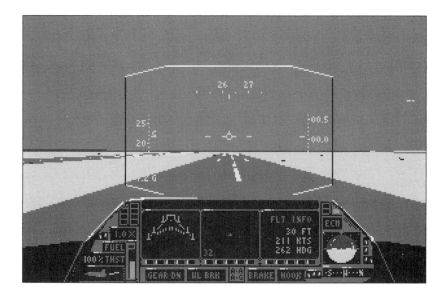

Figure 1-18. Flight path marker above the horizon on takeoff

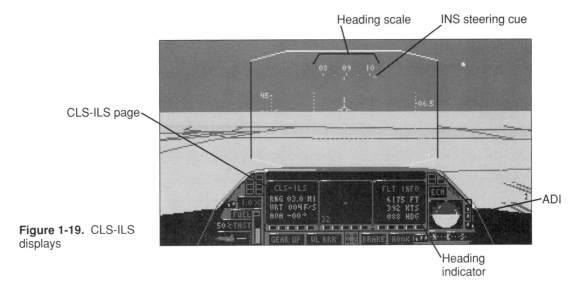

Figure 1-19. CLS-ILS displays

JetFighter Navigation

Next we will discuss JetFighter navigation. As we move along, note the heading scale at the top of the HUD. The numbers on this scale correspond to the aircraft heading. Another, less precise, heading scale is located in the lower-right corner of the cockpit. Both of these are shown in Figure 1-19. Also shown in the figure is the CLS-ILS page on the cockpit MMD. (The letters CLS-ILS stand for Carrier Landing System and Instrument Landing System.) At this time, call up the CLS-ILS page by pressing F1. When the CLS-ILS page is called up, an INS (Inertial Navigation System) steering cue (^) appears on the HUD heading scale. This cue is also shown in Figure 1-19. More on that later.

Turn to a heading of 090 degrees (which is 09 on the HUD heading scale). To accomplish this, roll the jet into a gentle bank with the joystick. Note that the horizon tilts as you make this maneuver. The cockpit ADI (Altitude Direction Indicator), located above the cockpit heading scale, will tilt the same amount as the horizon to show aircraft bank angle.

To perform a level turn, keep the flight path marker on the horizon as you turn. Also, in order to roll out at precisely 090 degrees, you must lead the roll out to wings level or stop turning and level off *before* you reach 090 degrees. So when the jet reaches 080 degrees, bank the aircraft to roll back to wings level.

Practice turning the jet to various headings. Once you can turn to a heading without embarrassing yourself too much, try rolling out on the INS steering cue, located on the HUD heading scale. As you follow this cue, you will notice that it will take you back to the airfield. This is true only in the CLS-ILS mode! An INS steering cue will also appear for bombing. This cue will take you to a designated target. (Bombing is a subject we'll discuss in great detail later.)

Stalls

Next up on the dance card is stalls. The first stall on the list is the *1 G stall*. To set up for this stall, place the flight path marker on the horizon and retard the throttle to 20 percent by pressing ②. As the airspeed rapidly decays, keep pulling back on the stick to keep the flight path marker on the horizon (and the aircraft in level flight). Remember our previous discussion of stalls. The AOA will keep increasing until stall AOA is reached. As you reach stall AOA, you'll get an audio stall warning tone and a flashing STALL indication on the cockpit Comm panel. The jet is shown in a stall in Figure 1-20. To recover from the stall, release the stick and let the nose fall toward the horizon while simultaneously hitting ⓪ to advance the power to 100 percent. As soon as the stall is broken, pull the nose back up.

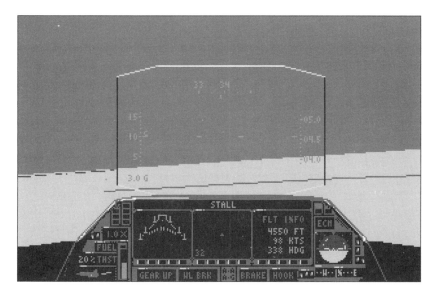

Figure 1-20. Cockpit view of an F-23 in a 1 *G* stall

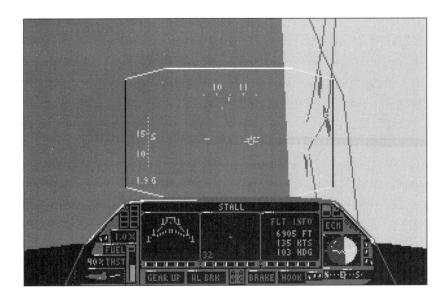

Figure 1-21. Cockpit view of an F-23 in an accelerated stall

This type of stall usually occurs when you're landing the jet, and you must react fast to keep the loss of altitude to a minimum.

You will notice that the F-23 has very benign stall characteristics. This is due to the swept wings. Swept-wing aircraft usually stall in a nose-up-to-level attitude rather than pitching down into a steep dive like a straight-wing aircraft. After a stall is entered, don't mistake a level or slightly nose high attitude as a recovery. To recover, you reduce the AOA by releasing back stick pressure while advancing the power. The F-23 is so powerful that you could probably just power out of the stall, but this is a bad stall recovery habit that will not work with jets that have less thrust available.

The next stall we will do is an *accelerated stall,* also called a high-speed stall. To enter an accelerated stall, make sure you're above 5000 feet and set the throttle to 40 percent. Next, enter a hard turn in either direction with the nose above the horizon. Keep pulling hard until you get a stall indication. Figure 1-21 shows the jet in an accelerated stall. When you hear the stall warning tone, immediately reduce back stick pressure and increase power by going to 100 percent. Again, the key to recovering from this stall is to reduce the AOA. In JetFighter, this stall usually occurs when you're fighting air-to-air and you may already be at full power. Note that during this type of stall the jet stalls at a higher airspeed.

After you practice a few stalls we'll move on to landings.

Landing

This section will discuss landing the jet. We will concentrate on setting up our approach and visually getting the aircraft on the runway or carrier safely. When flying in the JetFighter II Adventure it is useless to go out and accomplish your mission only to come back to the field or the boat and wrap the aircraft up into a pile of scrap metal. Takeoffs should equal landings as you fly and fight in JetFighter II.

   To set up for some landing practice:

1. Press [Esc] to call up the InFlight menus.
2. Select Free Flight and then the Land At option.
3. Once you are in the Land At option, select Los Angeles International Airport by pressing [Enter].

You'll immediately be transported to an aircraft on final approach at Los Angeles.

JetFighter Landing Symbology

Before we go over specific techniques, let's discuss the JetFighter cockpit and HUD landing symbology. Once you enter the cockpit, press [P] to pause the simulation. Figure 1-22 shows the F-23 cockpit and HUD. Note that the MMD (the left-hand cockpit CRT) has the

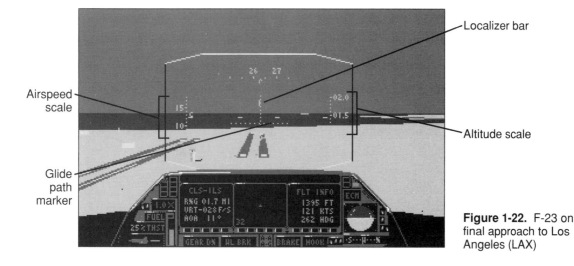

Figure 1-22. F-23 on final approach to Los Angeles (LAX)

letters CLS-ILS at the top of the display. More on that later, but for now let's go over the information provided by the MMD. With the CLS-ILS page called up, you get the following information:

RNG—range to the runway or carrier in miles.

VRT—vertical velocity, or your descent as measured in feet per second. This information is displayed in tens, so that -050 shows that the aircraft's vertical velocity is 500 feet per second down.

AOA—the aircraft's angle of attack.

On the right-hand CRT, which is also called the MFD, FLT INFO is displayed. This display provides the pilot with a digital readout of the aircraft's altitude, airspeed, and heading.

The F-23 HUD contains an airspeed scale on the far left side, a heading scale across the top, and an altitude scale on the far right side. *The most important display in the HUD for landing, however, is the flight path marker.* This display shows you the instantaneous aircraft path through the sky. You'll also notice the steering cue on the HUD heading scale, which we've already discussed. The thick vertical and horizontal dashed lines that are displayed in the HUD are part of the CLS-ILS system, which we'll discuss in detail in the next section. All of this symbology is shown in Figure 1-22.

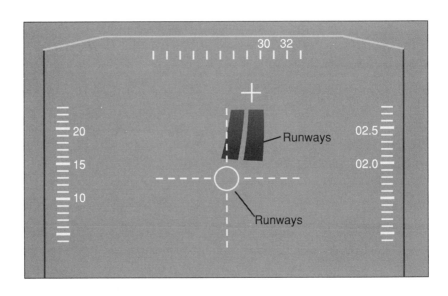

Figure 1-23. F-23 flight path marker on the runway threshold

Visual Landing Procedures

The Free Flight, Land At mode is an excellent way to perfect your landing techniques. Here's how you do it:

1. The first step upon entering the cockpit of the jet in flight is to lower the nose and place the flight path marker on the runway threshold (the end of the runway). Figure 1-23 shows this position. Leave the throttle at 25 percent for this approach and don't touch it.

2. Keep holding the flight path marker on the runway threshold as you descend. If you drift off your aim point in azimuth (side to side), make *small* bank angle changes to correct your course.

3. Cross-check your altitude on the right cockpit CRT. When you get to 200 feet, start a smooth flare by slowly pulling the nose up, which will slow your descent rate for landing. Figure 1-24 shows the jet in the flare just prior to touchdown. Be careful not to pull back on the stick too fast or you may stall the aircraft.

4. When you hear the jet touch down, bring the throttle to idle power by pressing ⌞˜⌟ or ⌞Tab⌟ or by holding down ⌞−⌟ until the RPM reads 0 percent.

5. Use the rudder (⌞Z⌟ or ⌞X⌟) to track straight down the runway. When you get to 50 knots of airspeed, press ⌞B⌟ to apply the wheel brakes.

Once you have mastered landing on runways, you can use the Free

Figure 1-24. F-23 in the flare just prior to touchdown

Flight menus to select a carrier for landing practice. The procedure for landing on a ship in JetFighter is the same, with the following exceptions: (1) Place the flight path marker on the aft end of the ship. When you get closer, you will see three wires on the deck. Put the flight path marker on the closest wire. (2) Don't flare. Just drive the jet right onto the deck.

Once you master landings using the computer to set you up on final approach, try taking off and setting yourself up for a landing. The next section covers flying an approach and landing without the aid of the Free Flight, Land At mode.

The Carrier Landing System—Instrument Landing System

The Carrier Landing System and the Instrument Landing System are virtually the same in JetFighter, so we'll just refer to this system as the ILS. Using the ILS is difficult at first, but once it is understood, landings and navigation are much easier to accomplish in JetFighter II. The first item to understand is the INS, or Inertial Navigation System. As we've discussed, the INS will provide the pilot with a steering cue, which is displayed on the HUD heading scale. This cue (^) appears when the pilot selects the CLS-ILS page on the MMD, and will provide steering to the airfield (or carrier) from which you took off. *It is important to understand that the INS steering cue in the HUD only provides steering directly from your present position to the airfield or carrier.* It does not tell you if you are on the right approach or if you are lined up with the correct runway. The only thing the steering cue tells you is that you are pointing at the airfield. You could be coming in from the wrong end of the airport, but the INS will still point *to* the airport. That is all it knows how to do.

The ILS steering bars give the pilot exact steering to get the jet on the runway. The vertical ILS bar, called the *localizer*, does help you figure out if you're coming in on a heading that will line you up for the correct runway, but it's a bit trickier to use. To get a handle on how a localizer works, imagine that the runway you want to land on has an imaginary extension that goes out in both directions for 30 miles. The localizer will tell you when you are *over* that imaginary extension of the runway. If you happen to pass over this imaginary extension of the runway, the localizer bar will slide to the center of the HUD. As you cross the extension and pass it, the localizer bar will move out of the center position to indicate that you are no longer

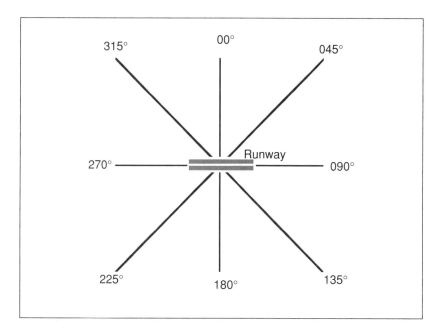

Figure 1-25. Radial (or spokes) off the landing runway

lined up. In essence, the localizer bar tells you when you are over the extension of the runway you wish to land on. *It does not tell you if you are pointed in the right direction.* You will need to use the INS for that. Be careful, because you could have the localizer bar centered and be pointing away from the airport!

If the localizer line is to the right of center in your HUD, that means that in order to pass over the imaginary extension of the runway, you will have to turn to the right a little, then fly straight until you get close to being above that imaginary line.

Figure 1-25 shows a useful way to picture this process. In this figure, imagine that your airport is at the center of a bicycle wheel, with spokes going out in all directions. One of these spokes will be aligned with the runway you're trying to land on. Using this diagram, we learn three important things:

- When your aircraft is pointing toward the center of the wheel, your INS pointer will be centered in the heading scale.

- When you are over the spoke that leads to your runway, the localizer bar will be centered in the HUD. Remember, you may not be facing toward the airport. All the localizer knows is that you are over the correct spoke.

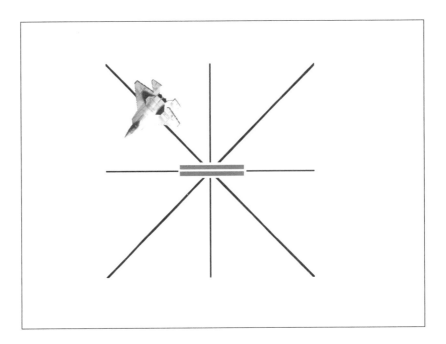

Figure 1-26. Arcing around to final approach

- When you're over the spoke *and* you are heading toward the airport, both the localizer bar and the INS pointer will be centered. You're on the glide path.

JetFighter also provides a Map view that can be very helpful in getting you lined up with the runway. In the next section we will discuss an approach and landing on a carrier, using all of JetFighter's available aids. All of these procedures also apply to landing on a runway.

Approach and Landing

In this discussion we'll assume that you're returning from a combat mission. These steps will get you back on deck or on the ground safely.

1. After deciding that you're going to RTB (return to base), press F1 to call up the CLS-ILS screen on the MMD.

2. Steer for the ship, using the HUD INS steering cue. When you get inside of 20 miles, power back to 30 percent and start your descent.

3. The optimum approach will start from 10 miles out and at 1500 feet. In order to get to the proper approach altitude of 1500 feet, keep pointing toward the ship (or runway), then when it comes into view, place the flight path marker short of the ship (or runway) to ensure that you will reach 1500 feet before you get to 10 miles. Start to level off at 2500 feet in order to get to your desired altitude of 1500 feet.

4. After leveling off, push the power up to 35 percent and keep steering directly toward the ship.

5. Select the Map view by pressing [M]. You can scale the Map view using the [,] and the [.] keys. The more you enlarge the map, the easier it will be to figure out your lineup with the ship (or runway). If you are within 45 degrees of the ship's heading, go to step 7. If not, keep flying straight in at the ship. When you get to 10 miles, start a turn away from the ship to fly a 10-mile arc or circle around the ship. Figure 1-26 show how we arc around the ship to get to our final approach course. Use the Map view to stay on the arc. The idea here is to fly the jet around on the arc until we are close to the extended runway or deck (represented by the vertical localizer steering line), then turn back into the ship to start our approach.

6. As you are arcing around the ship, when the localizer bar starts to move to the center of the HUD, start your turn into the ship to get lined up.

7. After rolling out of the turn, follow the localizer bar, and at 6 miles drop the gear ([G]) and the hook ([A]). It is not critical that you absolutely center this bar. If you are slightly off, just gently lean the jet into the localizer. Don't chase the bar or overcontrol. If you find yourself on Mister Toad's Wild Ride on final, roll wings level immediately and let things settle.

8. Power back to 30 percent.

Figure 1-27 shows the landing picture at 5 miles out.

9. The glide path bar will start to come down as you get in close (at about the 2-mile point). When this horizontal dashed line intersects the two solid horizontal lines in the HUD, power back to 27 percent and put the flight path marker on the aft end of the ship.

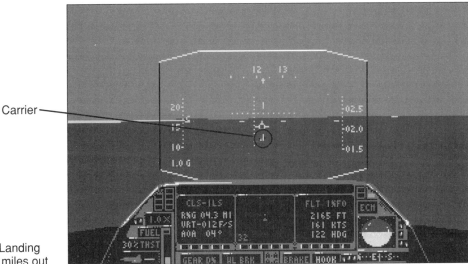

Figure 1-27. Landing picture from 5 miles out

10. When the wires on the deck come into view, place the flight marker on the closest wire and keep coming down until you impact the deck. Figure 1-28 shows this position.

11. As you hit the deck, go to full military power by pressing $\boxed{0}$. If you miss the wires (called a "bolter"), just take off again and come back around for another try. If you engage a wire, you'll be stopped and the mission will be over.

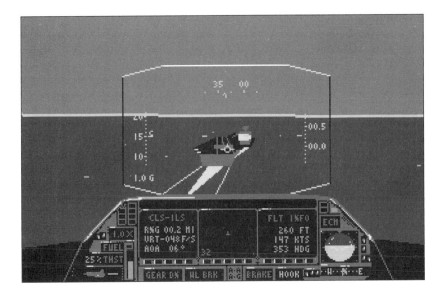

Figure 1-28. Landing picture with arresting wires in view

I know it's not easy landing this thing, but that's what makes it worth doing. Remember, kites can only rise against the wind; anything worth doing is worth doing well; and a stitch in time saves nine. Anyway, that's that for the training sortie. After perfecting the skills covered in this chapter, we're now ready to discuss one of my favorite subjects and the stuff that puts the fight in JetFighter—weapons.

2 Weapons

No plan survives the shock of battle.
—*Clausewitz,* On War

42

I was finishing up my checkout in the F-16C when this incident occurred. It was the kind of thing that could have happened to anybody, given the circumstances, but I was just glad that it didn't happen to me. The mission was briefed as a four-ship Surface Attack Tactics (SAT) ride to Echo Range in the Avon Park Range Complex in central Florida. A SAT ride is an air-to-ground mission where you go out and execute a multi-ship attack against a ground target, using a variety of ordnance. Today we were loaded with BDU-33 practice bombs. A BDU is a small 25-pound steel bomb with a spotting charge in it that goes off when it hits the ground. We carry BDUs because they have approximately the same ballistics as a real 500-pound general purpose bomb but they don't tear up the bombing range like a real bomb. When they come off the aircraft they're usually traveling at 800 feet per second, so they can still do a lot of damage to things they hit, but they obviously lack the wallop of 500 pounds of explosive. On this mission we'd planned to attack a bunkered command site near a runway complex on Echo Range. We planned to make six separate attacks for training purposes and drop one BDU on each pass.

The instructor pilot who was leading the mission was a new guy and hadn't been to this particular range. His briefing was mediocre at best, with a lot of time spent on things that everybody already knew and very little time spent finding the target (which we hadn't seen before). Going out the door to fly, I didn't think too much about our lack of target study because the picture of the range complex, which we'd glanced at in the briefing, showed a high-color-contrast runway on Echo Range with very distinct targets. Our target showed up as a nice white oval near the runway. A piece of cake to find and hit for the highly trained killer elite of the Top Dog Squadron.

We launched off the runway as singles and rejoined into a four-ship battle box formation. The low-level route started south of the range and then turned straight north toward the IP (Initial Point). We flew the 75-mile route without incident, and as we neared the IP

for the attack, the rear element dropped back from 2-mile trail to 5-mile trail. The IP is the reference point on the ground, between 8 and 15 miles out from the target, where the attack starts. As we approached the IP, I changed the weapon system from the air-to-air mode to an air-to-ground mode. The air-to-ground mode that I called up was Visual Release Point/Continuous Computing Release Point (VRP/CCRP) which we call "verp serp." In this mode the pilot can slew (move) an aiming reference in the HUD over a point on the ground (such as the IP), and update the attack steering to the target. Since the target is at a known bearing and distance from the IP, you can enter this mode and slew a diamond in the HUD over the IP. By slewing the diamond over the IP, you update the position of the IP in the fire control computer, which updates your steering to the target. As you approach the target, you'll get a cue in the HUD showing you where the target is located. This system is usually accurate to between 200 and 300 feet if you have good INS coordinates for the target and IP. This may sound like a large distance, but you don't use this mode to drop a bomb under normal circumstances. It just helps the pilot get his eyes on the target. Once you see the target, you switch to another, more accurate, mode to drop a bomb.

The IP on this mission was the west end of a bridge over a canal. I got a good slew on the IP, so I was confident that I could find the target. As we passed the IP we pushed it up to 540 knots for our run to the target. The attack we briefed was an Echelon Attack, with numbers 1 and 3 doing a 20-degree Low Angle Low Drag (LALD) pass and the wingman doing a Dive Toss pass on the target. I won't go into the whys and wherefores of this attack, but the mechanics are pretty simple. Both aircraft fly at the target at low altitude. At 4 miles from the target, you check 30 degrees away from the run-in heading (the heading you're on to fly to the target) and pull up to acquire the target. At a predetermined altitude, you pull back down and attack the target. The wingman just stays about a mile away from the leader and attacks the same target. On this mission I was flying as number 2 on the wing. I lined up 1 mile from the leader in a line-abreast position. We checked turned away from the target, and pulled up about 35 degrees nose high to acquire the target. As I pulled the jet down toward the target, I followed my HUD steering "verp serp" cue in order to pick up the target visually. My Target Designator (TD) box came smoothly into the HUD field of view, and as I looked through it to find the target I was amazed to find nothing but the green vegetation of central Florida beyond the nose of the jet.

There was nothing on the ground that I recognized from the picture in the briefing—and I mean nothing. Under my TD box should have been a nice white ploughed-out oval-shaped target. But as I stared glassy-eyed at my attack symbology, I saw not a single thing worth bombing in the HUD. Instead of panicking like some green lieutenant, I knew I had about 3 to 5 seconds to find the target, so with my pink body rushing toward the ground at 850 feet per second, I started to expand my search and look for the runway. My target was right next to the big runway. Surely I could spot a runway. How could you miss a runway complex? I expanded my gaze to find the runway, and soon realized there was no runway in my field of view. Like any experienced F-16 pilot, I know when to panic, and with 2 seconds left to decide what to do—this was the time. There was not a single target that looked like the target I had seen in the briefing. Well, it was now or never. I barely suppressed an urge to completely unravel at this point, and quickly came to the conclusion that the aircraft knew where it was and I didn't. After all, the F-16C is a state-of-the-art multi-million-dollar fighter aircraft. It must know where the target is—even if I was momentarily confused. Consistent with this line of thought, I lined up the VRP/CCRP steering in the HUD and pickled off (dropped) a BDU-33. As I pulled away from the target, I rolled up 110 degrees to spot my bomb impact and sure enough, it had hit in a mass of vegetation that didn't even look close to being the target area.

We left the target area and returned to the IP for another attack. On this mission we'd planned to make six attacks on the target and drop one bomb per pass. As we slowed down and headed back to the IP, I rechecked my air-to-ground weapons system to make sure that the fire control computer (FCC) and I were in sync. As we approached the IP, I could tell that everything was working correctly. There were only two possible explanations for this problem. The first was that both the weapon system and I were wrong. This was highly unlikely. The second was that the target area had changed since the pictures I'd seen were taken. This was possible, but as I set up for the next attack I wondered why it hadn't been covered in the briefing. We executed five more attacks. The next three went about the same as the first one. I kept dropping bombs using the FCC. Finally, on

the-next-to-last pass, I saw the target. It was about 300 feet to the south of where my bombs were falling, and was completely overgrown with bushes and tall grass. The runway was also barely visible under a carpet of thick green vegetation. This target didn't even come close to resembling the target photos we'd glanced at in the briefing, and consequently I'd missed it on four out of six passes.

Now for the really interesting part of the story. The other two-ship that was part of our flight was also attacking the same targets, but was 5 miles behind us. They completed all their attacks and we returned to MacDill AFB as a four-ship.

After landing we sat in the debrief, and every one of us had trouble identifying the target area. In a debriefing it is customary to review each pilot's film of the first attack, so we started out by watching the VTR film of number 1's first attack. It turned out he had actually found the target and successfully attacked it. We put my film in next, and found out that I'd attacked some shrubs 300 feet away from the target area. Number 3 said his film hadn't run. Yeah, sure. But we didn't press the issue, and we moved on to number 4's film.

Four's film proved to be very interesting from the start. As the tape rolled, I noticed immediately that he wasn't following his "verp serp" steering to the target as he pulled down. Once he did pull down, his HUD was filled with what appeared to be a target area that looked like the picture we'd seen in the briefing. A nice ploughed-out line stood out in the HUD field of view, along with a number of very distinct targets. In a few seconds, however, a sinking feeling swept through the briefing room as the flight recognized this "target area" that number 4 was attacking was the *manned,* I repeat *manned,* conventional range. The conventional range, called the Charlie Range, has occupied observation towers that are used to control conventional bombing events. On a conventional range, you bomb an easy-to-find bullseye target from a very tightly controlled run-in direction. People are usually working in and around the towers on a conventional range because the bomb impacts are on these bullseye targets. Charlie Range is located about 2 miles away from the Echo tactical range we were supposed to be bombing. We watched the film in horror as this knuckle-futz in our flight dove at the ground, hurling bombs at a spot probably occupied by non-combatant, freedom-loving American citizens (and probably Republicans).

The flight lead immediately jumped up from his seat and hit the pause button on the tape machine, freezing number 4's bombing pass on the TV monitor. He then turned to number 4 with a pleading look on his face. With the fear in his voice that can only come from a young man about to be hung by the thumbs, he said, "Tell me you didn't actually drop a bomb on this pass."

A silence hung over the briefing room. Number 4 answered the question with his silence, gazing forlornly off into space. A groan went up from the rest of us as we realized that 25-pound bullets, moving 800 feet per second, had been launched near "friendlies." We all looked at each other, hoping that Scotty would "beam us up" or that maybe divine intervention would save the day in some way or other. It took only a moment to realize that this problem was not going to go away. The leader pressed the pause button again and the tape continued. Number 4 dove toward the center tower on Charlie Range with evil intent and let fly a BDU-33 about 100 feet from the center range tower. There was little consolation in the fact that no scurrying figures appeared in the HUD. We let the tape roll on and sat in silence, watching with an ever-increasing feeling of foreboding. Five more passes produced five more attacks on Charlie Range. The bombs all fell in and around the center tower. After the last pass, the flight lead turned off the VTR and sat back down.

I was the most experienced and senior member of the flight so I thought it was my place to say a few words at this time. I pointed out that since Charlie Range had not made a radio call during this attack, maybe there was nobody on the range. I also pointed out that we hadn't received a phone call from range control either, and I added jokingly that we hadn't been met by the Wing Commander with the Security Police when we landed, so we probably hadn't killed anybody, and even if we had, nobody knew about it yet. Nobody laughed as the flight lead rose to go get the Squadron Commander and show him the tape of the attack.

No need to go any farther into this tale except to say that the story had a happy ending. Luck was with us that day and Charlie Range was clear during number 4's attack. A half hour before we showed up on the range, several people were in and around the range tower working, but they had left by the time we arrived. We all skated on this one, and even number 4 got only a mild chewing out (along with a whole lot of supervision for several months following the incident).

The moral of the story is simple—in order to successfully employ a modern fighter aircraft you need to know your weapons system inside and out. Number 4 didn't know his weapons system well enough. If he had followed his "verp serp" steering he would have avoided attacking the wrong target. In this chapter we will discuss JetFighter II weapons and related cockpit and HUD cues. This information is important to the JetFighter pilot, and will prevent buffoonery in the simulation.

JETFIGHTER WEAPONS

The JetFighter II simulation has three basic classes of weapons: guided air-to-air missiles, unguided projectiles, and free-fall bombs. For each weapon class there are unique cockpit and HUD displays. JetFighter II is very easy to employ as a weapons system because there are only three classes of weapons, each with its own unique HUD presentations for employing the weapons in that class. Within each class of weapon there may be several specific types of weapons, but all weapons in a class are aimed and fired the same way. The only differences between weapons types in a given class are their effective range and some other minor performance features. The following list shows the JetFighter II weapons:

AIR-TO-AIR MISSILES

AIM-9L Sidewinder

AIM-120 AMRAAM

AIM-54 Phoenix

UNGUIDED PROJECTILES

M61A1 20-mm Gun

AIM-166 Kinetic Energy Missile
    (really an unguided rocket)

FREE-FALL BOMBS

Mark-82 500-lb General Purpose Bomb

Mark-84 2000-lb General Purpose Bomb

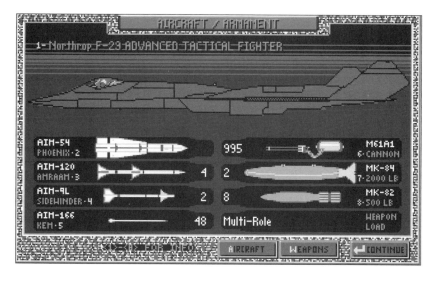

Figure 2-1. JetFighter II weapons page

Figure 2-1 shows the JetFighter II weapons page with the available weapons for each aircraft and mission selected. By changing the aircraft or mission load-out you can change the weapons configuration for your mission. Not all weapons are available for all aircraft and missions. If you cycle through the selections, you will notice that the weapons numbers change. Later in the book, when we cover mission planning, we'll discuss how to select various weapons loads. For now, we'll discuss each weapon used in JetFighter II.

The only missiles used in JetFighter II are air-to-air missiles. They all have slightly different range characteristics, but they all share the same cockpit and HUD symbology. The missiles used in JetFighter II are the AIM-9L Sidewinder, the AIM-120 AMRAAM, and the AIM-54 Phoenix. The AIM-166 has the word "missile" in its name, but it is not a missile at all. This weapon is an unguided rocket and we'll discuss it later.

JETFIGHTER II AIR-TO-AIR MISSILES

JetFighter II Missile Characteristics

The JetFighter missiles guide on enemy fighters when fired within the proper weapons envelope. Guided air-to-air missiles in JetFighter II work on the same fundamental principle as they do in the real world. The pilot flies the jet into a position on the target that is within the proper launch envelope for the selected air-to-air missile. He then fires the missile, which guides on the target and detonates when the fuze detects that the target is within the missile warhead's range. The warhead goes boom and destroys the target. These three steps—guidance, fuze function, and warhead detonation—must all be successful in order to destroy the target. In the history of air combat there have been several engagements in which a missile has come out of the jet, guided on the enemy aircraft, and failed to fuze while passing close to the target. There is nothing a pilot can do about these situations, so in JetFighter it is always better to launch two missiles per target to ensure a kill. In JetFighter II, the AMRAAM and the Phoenix are radar-guided missiles, while the Sidewinder is an infrared, or IR, guided missile. The only difference in employing these missiles in JetFighter is that their effective ranges differ.

	Min Range	Max Range
AIM-91L Sidewinder	.5 miles	5 miles
AIM-120 AMRAAM	.5 miles	10 miles
AIM-54 Phoenix	1 mile	15 miles

JetFighter II Air-to-Air Missile Symbology

Figure 2-2 shows the F-23 cockpit and HUD display with a Sidewinder called up. To call up a missile in the simulation you press [Enter]. The selected weapon will change and this will be visible in the left MMD weapons display. In order to get this display up in the left MMD, press [F1] until an icon of the aircraft wing appears in the left MMD. You can think of this display as the JetFighter armament or stores management panel. You get to the panel with [F1] and you cycle through the weapon choices on the panel with [Enter]. As you press [Enter], the selected weapon will appear below the word ARM on the display.

In the HUD, you will get a missile reticle (which is nothing more than a circle) when you call up an air-to-air missile. In addition you will get a TD box, or Target Designator box, around an enemy aircraft when you're locked onto a target that is inside the HUD field of view. The TD box helps get your eyes on target. It has nothing directly to do with shooting a missile. The next thing you will see in

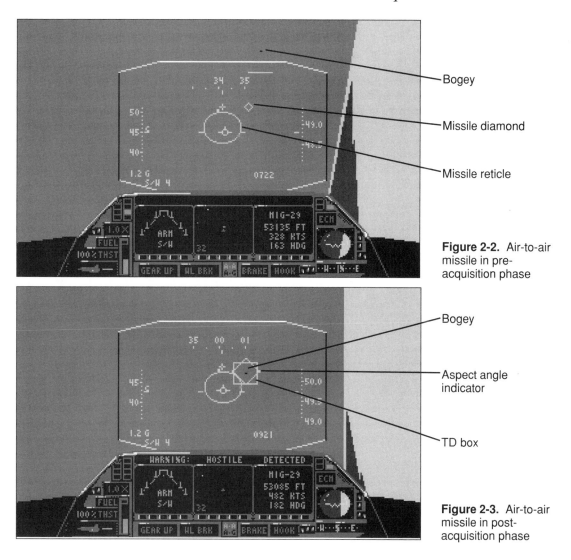

Figure 2-2. Air-to-air missile in pre-acquisition phase

Figure 2-3. Air-to-air missile in post-acquisition phase

the HUD is a missile diamond. The missile diamond is your key HUD aiming device for a missile shot in JetFighter. The diamond appears in the HUD when the target you're locked onto is in the HUD field of view. The diamond stays small until the selected missile acquires the target. When this occurs, the diamond jumps to a larger size and you get a change in audio to denote missile seeker lock-on. In Figure 2-2 the missile diamond is in the pre-acquisition phase. In Figure 2-3 the missile has acquired the target and the diamond has jumped to its post-acquisition size, indicating missile lock-on to the target.

Aspect Angle

There is one other important indicator that appears in the HUD when a missile is selected. This is the aspect angle indicator. The aspect mark is nothing more than a small box that appears on the missile reticle, showing target aspect. Figure 2-4 shows various target aspects and what the JetFighter pilot will see in the HUD when looking at the missile reticle.

In the next chapter, when we discuss maneuvering air combat and tactical intercepts, the word "aspect" will be used a number of times, so make sure you understand it. Target aspect can be confusing, but it is simply a measure of the direction from the target's tail to your aircraft. If the aspect indicator is at dead 6 o'clock on the missile reticle, than the bandit is showing you tail aspect. You are looking at the target's tail, so he is headed away from you. If the aspect indicator is at the 12 o'clock position, you're looking straight down the "snot locker" on the bandit (he is headed straight at you). If the aspect angle indicator is at the 3 o'clock or 9 o'clock position, then you're looking down the wing line of the bandit and he is 90 degrees out from your heading. You can see why aspect is so important. It instantly tells you your relationship to the bandit. In JetFighter II you can only be locked to one bandit at a time, so you'll only be getting aspect on one bandit.

Figure 2-4. Target aspect as shown on the missile reticle

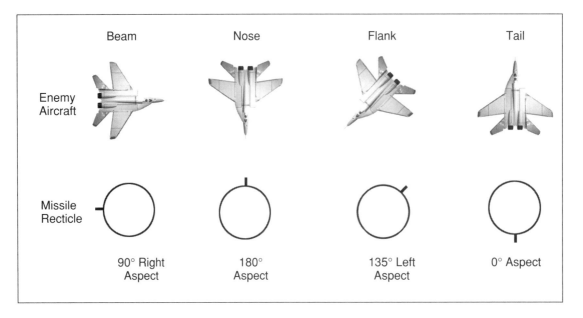

Other Related Missile Symbology

Also appearing on the missile reticle is a range marker, which slides around to show range from the target in 1000-foot increments. This marker is very useful in helping you determine your range from a target that you're locked onto with your radar. To determine your range to the target using this marker, just take the clock position of the range marker on the missile reticle and multiply by 1000 feet. Figure 2-5 shows the marker at 6 o'clock, which indicates a target at 6000 feet from your aircraft.

In addition to the range marker, the HUD shows an IN RNG, or "in range," cue in its lower-right corner. This cue will flash when the target that you are locked onto is within range of the weapon you have selected.

Shooting a Missile in JetFighter II

Now we know about JetFighter missile symbology, let's discuss firing a missile in the simulation. There are several steps that must be accomplished in order to fire a missile successfully. These steps will ensure that you are in the envelope of the missile, and will give you the best chance of having your missile guide, fuze, and destroy the target.

1. **Get your cockpit displays set up correctly.**
   - **Right MFD**—press F2 until AIR TARG appears.
   - **Center HSD**—press R to adjust scope size to the smallest size that will still keep the target on the scope.
   - **Left MFD**—press F1 until the stores management panel appears.

2. **Select the missile that you want to shoot.**

   Your selection of the missile is usually dependent on the range to the target. Normally, flying the F-23, you'll want to shoot an AMRAAM first and, when you get closer, switch to a Sidewinder. If you're flying an F-14 or F-18, you may have a Phoenix loaded. In that case you would fire it first, followed by the AMRAAM and the Sidewinder as the range to the target decreases.

   To select the appropriate missile, press Enter until the desired missile appears on the left MFD. Note that if you pass the missile you want, you'll have to cycle through all the available weapons on the weapons rotary to get back to it. When selecting a weapon in JetFighter, it's best to take your time.

3. **Lock onto the target.**

   To do this, press ⊤ until the target you want to shoot flashes on the center HSD. A target that you're locked onto and tracking with your radar will flash on the HSD, while the right MMD will display the target's altitude, airspeed, and heading.

4. **Fly the target into the HUD field of view.**

   This can be very difficult for the novice JetFighter pilot, but you must get a handle on this key step in order to employ air-to-air missiles successfully. The easiest way to do this is to fly your jet to the target's altitude (which you can read off the right MFD). Next, place the target on the nose by turning the jet to line up the flashing square in the HSD (which is the target that you are locked onto) right at the 12 o'clock position. If you are within 200 to 330 feet of the target's altitude and have placed the flashing target square in the HSD at the 12 o'clock position, you'll soon get the target in the HUD, as shown in Figure 2-5. When the target appears in the HUD you'll get a TD box and a small diamond. When the diamond jumps to the larger size, the missile is tracking the target. All you have to do now is make sure that you're in range and shoot the missile (by pressing Spacebar or the #1 button on your joystick).

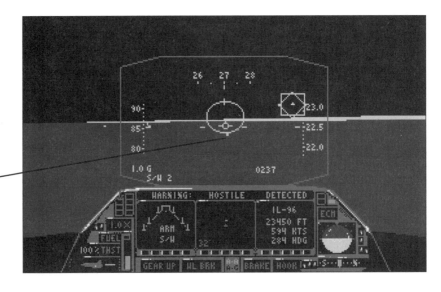

Range marker

Figure 2-5. Aircraft target in the HUD

JetFighter II missile symbology is very straightforward and easy to use. What is more difficult is actually lining up the target and keeping it in the HUD. In the next chapter we will discuss JetFighter air-to-air techniques in greater detail.

JetFighter II features two different types of unguided weapons that can be shot (as opposed to dropped) from the aircraft. These weapons are the M61A1 20-mm cannon and the AIM-166 Kinetic Energy Missile. They can be used for all air targets and a few selected ground targets. Both of these weapons use the same HUD symbology, and they fire from the jet in a similar way. The first and most useful JetFighter projectile weapon is the 20-mm gun.

JETFIGHTER II UNGUIDED PROJECTILES

THE JetFighter II 20-MM CANNON

The JetFighter cannon is a 20-mm Gatling gun that fires approximately 100 high-explosive incendiary rounds per second. These bullets are small, but very effective against thin-skinned targets such as aircraft and trucks. When the gun is fired, these bullets fly straight out of the jet and are affected only by gravity and friction. Gravity pulls the bullet toward the ground and friction slows the projectile over time. These bullets are unguided, so the pilot has to fly the jet into the correct position on the target in order to get a hit. The 20-mm gun is a very short-range weapon compared to the missiles in JetFighter II, and is used primarily when you are in too close for a missile shot.

JetFighter 20-mm Gun Symbology

The 20-mm gun is primarily an air-to-air weapon, so when it is called up on the stores management panel in the left MMD, an air-to-air optimized aiming cue appears in the HUD. This cue, shown in Figure 2-6, is essentially a simplified Lead Computing Optical Sight, or LCOS (pronounced el-coss). This sight tells the pilot where the 20-mm gun is currently aimed, given the present relationship between the shooter and the target. Gun-aiming theory is not simple, but fortunately it is not necessary to understand it in order to shoot the gun in JetFighter. All you need to know is that you place the aiming reference over the target and shoot when you're in gun range.

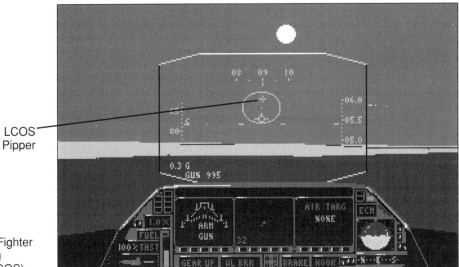

Figure 2-6. JetFighter Lead Computing Optical Sight (LCOS)

The LCOS pipper (or aiming cue) will move straight up and down as you and the target change flight conditions (*G*s, airspeed, nose position in relation to the horizon, etc.). This movement is present in order to indicate to the pilot the proper amount of lead (aim in front of the target) for the gun shot. Shooting an enemy aircraft with the gun is basically the same as shooting clay pigeons. Because the projectiles must fly unguided toward the target, the shooter must pull lead, or lead the target, in order to achieve a hit. The LCOS pipper will depress (move closer to the bottom of the HUD) in order to help the pilot aim farther out in front of the target. This movement may be subtle and hard for the pilot to discern. All you have to do to hit the target with the gun is put the LCOS pipper over the target and shoot.

Shooting the Gun in JetFighter II

There are three steps to a gun shot in JetFighter II.

1. **Call up the gun on the left MMD stores management display.**
   You press F1 to get to this display, and then press Enter to cycle through the weapons rotary and get to the 20-mm gun.

2. **Point the jet out in front of the target and get within gun range.**
   A gun shot can be difficult to make against a maneuvering target, because in order to shoot the bullet and have it rendezvous with

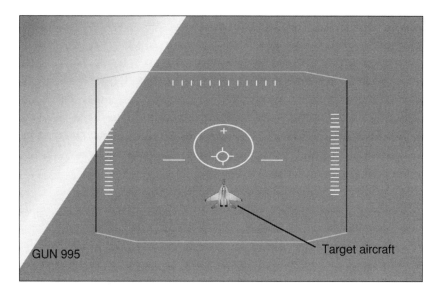

GUN 995

Target aircraft

Figure 2-7. Flight path marker in front of the target

the target, you must predict the target's motion through the sky. This is not an easy task, but the best way to accomplish it is to put the flight path marker out in front of the target, as shown in Figure 2-7.

3. **Open fire with Spacebar or with the #1 button on your joystick.** In JetFighter, you should shoot in short bursts. Remember to lead the target when you shoot.

The AIM-166 Kinetic Energy Missile

The Kinetic Energy Missile, or KEM, is a new weapon to JetFighter II. Also known as a Hyper Velocity Rocket, the KEM can be thought of as a slow-firing gun with a better range. The 20-mm cannon is a good, cheap general-purpose weapon, but it has many drawbacks in aerial gunnery. The primary drawback, of course, is the limited range of the 20-mm projectile. In JetFighter II, the KEM is aimed and fired exactly like the 20-mm gun, but its range is greater. On the negative side, you're carrying a limited number of these weapons, so you can't fire at the same rate as you can with the 20-mm gun.

The JetFighter KEM travels at a much higher speed than either the cannon round or the air-to-air missiles. Because of its high speed, the rocket experiences little gravity drop after launch. The effects of gravity are felt by ballistic projectiles as a function of their time in flight, but a KEM rocket moves so fast that the effects of gravity are negligible. A KEM round is typically made of depleted uranium, a very dense and heavy substance. Because such a dense projectile is traveling at such a high velocity, a hit—even in a non-vital area of an enemy aircraft—is almost surely lethal. A KEM round is about 1.5 inches in diameter and 4 feet long. At the tip is the depleted uranium projectile, and at the end is the rocket motor that propels the missile. A KEM does not need a warhead; it uses impact with the target as the kill mechanism.

Shooting the KEM in JetFighter II

In JetFighter, the KEM can be used against enemy fighters, but the low fire rate is a real disadvantage against a maneuvering target. Against Cruise missiles or other non-maneuvering targets it is a reasonably good weapon. In JetFighter II the KEM should be aimed and fired exactly like the 20-mm cannon, with one important exception. You don't need to lead the target as much, because this is a very fast projectile. In fact, when you get within about 3000 feet of the target you can just point straight at the target and shoot.

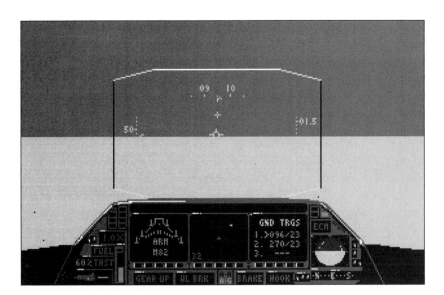

Figure 2-8. Mark 82 General Purpose Bomb Selected

KEM can also be used against ground targets. We'll discuss using the KEM and the 20-mm gun on ground targets in the air-to-ground chapter.

The JetFighter II simulation has only one class of air-to-ground weapons. This class is the good old dumb bomb. There is not much to understand about this type of weapon. The pilot pickles (releases) the bomb; it falls toward the ground in accordance with Newton's Laws and goes boom. While these bombs are simple in concept, they are very difficult to employ. Dumb bombs require very smart flying in order to hit the target. There are no computer brains at work here helping you figure the proper release conditions or guiding the weapon toward the target. Figure 2-8 shows the cockpit and HUD symbology that are present when you have a Mark-82 or Mark-84 bomb called up. You'll notice that there's not much there in the way of aiming cues. Because dropping free-fall bombs without the aid of a computer system is so difficult, we'll talk about dropping Mark-82 500-pound and Mark-84 2000-pound bombs in great detail in the air-to-ground chapter of this book (Chapter 4).

FREE-FALL BOMBS

3 Air Combat Maneuvering

When the strike of the hawk breaks the body of its prey, it is because of timing.
—*Sun Tzu,* The Art of War *(500 B.C.)*

It was one of those missions that I knew was going to turn out bad from the start. My fighter squadron was converting from the A-7D to the F-16C, and this was one of my last rides in the old Corsair II. On this sortie we were scheduled to fly a Four versus Four DACT (Dissimilar Air Combat Tactics) engagement against two Hornets (F-18s) and two Turkeys (F-14s) that were going to launch from the deck of the U.S.S. America, just off the coast of North Carolina. The briefing went well, but only served to highlight the fact that we were dead meat out there against jets that had Pulse Doppler radar, better weapons (Aim-7s and Aim-9s against our Aim-9s), and much better maneuverability. I left the squadron in a funk to go out and strap on the jet, resolving not to feel too bad about getting slaughtered on this mission. As I approached the aircraft, I noticed that the A-7 I was scheduled to fly had two wing-mounted fuel tanks loaded. This couldn't be right. We never flew air-to-air with wing tanks in the A-7, or in any fighter I'd ever flown, with the exception of the F-4. In the F-4 it didn't mattered much, since you were already flying a cinderblock with wings. In the A-7 it mattered a lot. The crew chief informed me that this was the correct configuration because the aircraft was going on its last flight to the boneyard the next day and needed the wing tanks for the trip to Arizona. Great— not only did I have to fight F-14s and F-18s in an A-7, I had to fight them in an A-7 on its last operational flight that was configured with wing tanks. The A-7 is not known for having great maneuverability when it's clean, much less when you're hauling the equivalent of two Volkswagen Beetles under each wing. Well, it was better than not flying at all—but not much better.

Takeoff and climb-out were uneventful, and in a few minutes our four-ship was "feet wet" (over water), talking to the Air Boss on the America. Soon the E-2C Hawkeye was shot off the Cat (catapult), and we checked in with him and got set up to fight. The E-2C's job was to provide radar coverage for both sides during the engagement and to pass shots back and forth between the flights, since our flight of A-7s was using a different UHF frequency from the F-14s and F-

18s. By using separate frequencies you avoid garbaging up the other side's communications; also, you can't eavesdrop on their radio calls. The problem of two separate frequencies is that you can't hear the other side calling shots on you, and vice versa. That's where the E-2C (or a ground-based controller) comes in. They listen to both frequencies and pass the shots back and forth. Because we don't use real missiles, you have to call in your simulated shots on the radio.

The Navy fighters followed the Hawkeye off the deck of the carrier and the fight got started with a 30-mile setup. Our game plan was to stay together as a four-ship and react defensively to the medium-range radar missile (Aim-7) by using range calls from the Hawkeye. The enemy fighters came directly at us as expected. At predetermined range (based on the radio transmissions of the E-2C), our flight of four A-7s maneuvered aggressively away from the Navy jets to defeat their missile shots. We held this new course for less than a minute, then turned back into the F-14s. This maneuver seemed to fool the enemy slightly, because when we came out of the turn and pointed toward them, the range was less than 5 miles and they had only called one of us dead. As we merged (entered a visual fight), I picked up sight of an F-14 turning on me and closing rapidly from the 8 o'clock position. I had good knots on the jet (for an A-7) and turned left into him at about 7 *G*s. He tightened up his turn to stay behind me, but couldn't hack the corner, so he grossly overshot high and right and came out at my 4 o'clock. I glanced quickly at my airspeed and noticed that I still had 380 knots, so I executed an unloaded reversal to the right back into the F-14. As I rolled right, I noticed that the Turkey had his wings spread full forward and was starting a zoom in the vertical, expecting me to quickly run out of energy and fall off. You can always tell a Turkey's airspeed by his wings and when they're forward, he's slow. Because I knew he was slow and because I still had good knots, I pulled into the vertical with him and we went straight up, canopy-to-canopy.

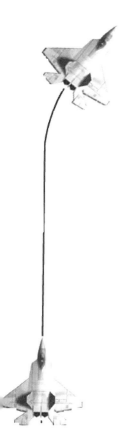

The Turkey is not a very well-powered aircraft compared to a modern fighter, but it is better than an A-7. The F-14 is currently in the process of getting more powerful engines, but getting new engines for the Turkey is like putting racing silks on a mule. Even with these engines, the F-14 TomTurkey is just too big and heavy to maneuver like a real fighter. Fortunately for this Turkey pilot, I wasn't flying a real fighter. Even so, at this point in time and space I was staying right with him. The 100 knots of airspeed I had on him at the start of the zoom helped. As we climbed straight up, I arched my head way back to look out of the very top of the canopy and sure enough, through the F-14 canopy, I saw two sets of helmets and dark visors staring back at me. I knew that a tanked A-7 going nose high with a Turkey was a sight these guys had never seen before. Because of the size of the F-14, it felt like I was zooming with a 727.

Well, it was glorious while it lasted but it didn't last for long. As the jet started to get slow, I started to rudder the nose of the old bird back down toward the Atlantic. There was no need to get down to zero airspeed, because by this time the F-14 had climbed above me and was still nose high and staying there. This was going to be a lost cause no matter what I did, so I figured I might as well keep the jet going through the sky with the pointy end first. No need to flirt with a departure. I got the nose going straight down and saw the F-14 coming down after me in my 6 o'clock position to finish me off. Just as I was getting ready to begin a guns jink-out (a maneuver to avoid getting shot by a gun), the E-2C controller came onto the radio and called, "Fox-2 kill on the F-14 at 28,000 nose high with the A-7." I couldn't believe it. One of my wingmen had killed this guy with a simulated Aim-9 Sidewinder shot (Fox-2) before he could pull down on top of me. Zooming the A-7, wing tanks and all, had worked because it had bought me some time. Unfortunately, this nose high slow fight had attracted a Hornet, which by the way is a great fighter in every respect. He casually pointed at my wallowing Corsair and stuck me with a Sidewinder, and that was that for this engagement.

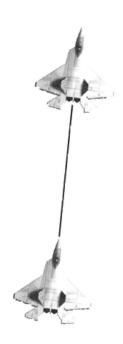

We ended up fighting two more engagements against these guys, and since there is no way I can tell you how the rest of these fights went without using profanity, I'll stop right here on a high note. This first Four versus Four fight went a lot better than I had expected, and reinforced a fighter axiom that I knew all along—air-to-air combat always surprises you. Every single fight is different, and the outcomes are not always predictable. In this chapter, we'll cover techniques for shooting things down in the JetFighter simulation. I have found that air-to-air engagements in a real jet fighter and air-to-air engagements in the JetFighter II simulation share this trait of unpredictability. Our discussion in this chapter will cover some fundamental air-to-air terminology and techniques that are used both when burning jet fuel and when burning electricity from your wall socket. With this knowledge, you can react successfully to the unpredictable air-to-air combat situations that you'll encounter in JetFighter II.

BASIC FIGHTER MANEUVERS (ONE VERSUS ONE AIR COMBAT)

Basic fighter maneuvers, or BFM, are the foundation of all fighter maneuvering. There is no doubt that you can blunder around the sky in JetFighter II without knowing BFM fundamentals. However, there is no way to execute the missions in JetFighter II with style unless you have some BFM knowledge. Style is important to a fighter pilot because "style" is a word that implies disciplined execution of the basics. You strap the jet on and you execute the mission with precision and consistency based on established tactics and techniques. I'll give you a start on understanding modern fighter tactics and air combat techniques. By executing your JetFighter II missions with style, you'll be flying sorties the way fighter pilots are currently flying real missions and, more important, you'll be more successful and achieve a higher skill level in the simulation. Fighter pilots always encounter unexpected tactical situations, both in the real world and in JetFighter II, but if they're knowledgeable and disciplined they can react successfully to these encounters. Success for a fighter pilot is simply defined: kill the enemy and survive. Well, enough of the "why" part of this discussion; it's time to move on to "how."

Basic fighter maneuvers are nothing more than the art of exchanging energy for aircraft position. Energy, for the purpose of our discussion, is fighter speed and altitude. *Offensive maneuvering* in the simulation (or in a real fighter) has a single purpose: to fly your jet into a position to shoot your weapons at the bandit. In *defensive maneuvering* your purpose is to fly your jet into a position where the bandit can't fire his weapons at your aircraft. In *head-on maneuvering* you must get behind the bandit from a neutral position. When you execute maneuvers to accomplish these objectives you'll invariably bleed off, or expend, energy. Pulling *G*s and turning cause all aircraft to lose energy (which means that altitude and airspeed drop). In JetFighter II, when you select the F-23 you'll notice that it does not display these normal fighter characteristics. This is because the jet has so much thrust that it always has plenty of energy (which can be thought of as maneuvering potential). Even though this is true of the F-23, the basic BFM principles of offensive, defensive, and head-on maneuvering still apply. In this discussion of BFM we will describe the geometry of the fight and the specific maneuvers that you need to know. Even though you're flying a high-energy machine, geometry is geometry, as you will soon see.

Flying in the Future

Many discussions of BFM overemphasize canned maneuvers. They discuss these maneuvers as if they were game pieces that you could play *after* an opponent makes his move. You may have seen documentation that shows the obligatory Yo-Yos and other supposed air-to-air maneuvers that you fly in an engagement. These moves are described in great detail, and some people even write about situations where they can be used. Most of this stuff is entertaining to read, but not very useful once you start mixing it up. Air-to-air combat is not a setpiece game, but rather a fluid contest of quick reaction, with both opponents executing a blur of moves and countermoves. The JetFighter simulation may have taught you by now that you are definitely in a fluid and dynamic fight, with little room for creative thought or careful analysis. Aerial combat requires reaction. Nobody has ever accused fighter pilots of being brilliant. Analyzing potentially dangerous, changing conditions and surviving them is a unique skill fighter pilots must have, though. In air-to-air maneuvering, the decision process can be broken down into four steps:

1. **Observe** the bandit.
2. **Predict** a future position in space for the bandit based on your observation.
3. **Maneuver** your jet in response to this prediction.
4. **React** to changes in the situation as you execute your maneuvers.

This list shows that BFM is flown in the future and not in the present. You must constantly predict the bandit's future position, a few seconds from the time you observe him, and fly your jet based on this prediction. A fighter pilot normally does not have time to observe a situation and, based on a future prediction, execute a classic BFM maneuver. Normally in JetFighter II (as in a real fighter), you will have to execute quick high-*G* turns in rapid succession. More on that later. Before we get into that discussion we should talk about the geometry of the fight.

Spatial Relationships

In order to fly BFM correctly, a fighter pilot must understand his spatial relationship to the target from four perspectives: positional geometry, attack geometry, the weapon envelope, and the control zone.

Positional Geometry

Range, aspect angle, and *angle-off* (heading crossing angle, or HCA) are the terms used to describe one aircraft's position relative to another. These terms, illustrated in Figure 3-1, are said to define the angular relationship between two aircraft. This angular relationsip is a detailed way of defining two fighters' positions in space and is used to show relative advantage or disadvantage in air-to-air combat.

Figure 3-1. Positional geometry

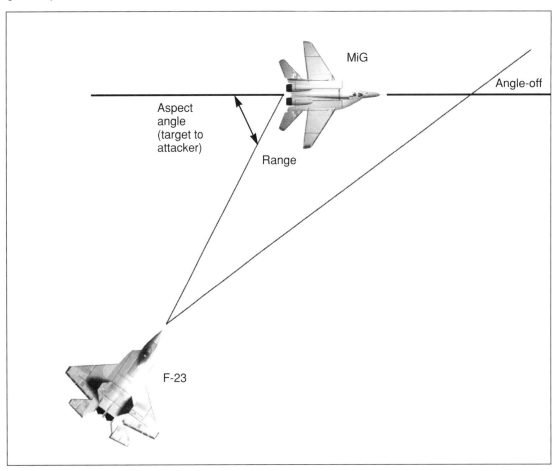

Range is the distance, measured in feet or nautical miles, between your jet and the enemy fighter.

Aspect angle is the number of degrees measured from the tail of the target to your aircraft. Aspect angle is important because it tells you how far away you are in degrees from directly behind the stern of the target (the desired position).

Angle-off is the difference, measured in degrees, between your heading and the bandit's. This angle tells you how much your fuselage is aligned with the bandit's fuselage. For example, if the angle-off were 0 degrees, you would be on a parallel heading with the bandit and your fuselage would be aligned with his. If the angle-off were 90 degrees, your fuselage would be perpendicular to the bandit's.

Attack Geometry

Attack geometry describes the nose position of your jet relative to the bandit. When you start an attack on the bandit, there are three distinct paths, or pursuit courses, available. These pursuit courses are *pure pursuit, lag pursuit,* and *lead pursuit.* If you're pointing directly at the bandit, you're flying a pure pursuit course. If you're pointing behind the bandit, you're in lag pursuit. If your nose is out in front of the bandit, you're in lead pursuit. Figure 3-2 shows these three pursuit options. In the JetFighter simulation you can tell what pursuit course you're flying by the position of the flight path marker in relation to the bandit. Figure 3-3 shows

Figure 3-2. Pursuit options

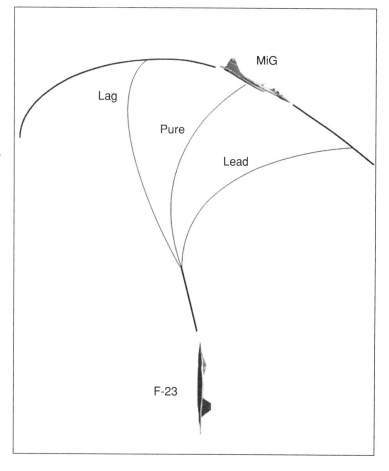

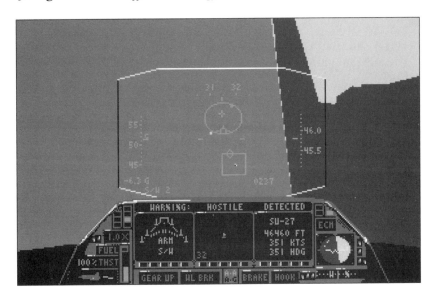

Figure 3-3. Lead pursuit course as seen from the cockpit

a lead pursuit course with the flight path marker in front of the bandit. In pure pursuit, the flight path marker would be right over the bandit and if you were flying a lag pursuit course, the flight path marker would be behind him.

The Weapons Envelope

The weapons envelope is the area near the bandit where you can fire a weapon and destroy him. It is defined by range, aspect angle, and angle-off. The dimensions of this area are determined by the types of weapons loaded on your jet. If your jet is carrying all-aspect Aim-9Ls or Aim-120s, this area around the bandit looks like a doughnut, whose inside line in the minimum range (Rmin) and whose outside line is the maximum range (Rmax). Figure 3-4 shows a shaded doughnut area, which represents the weapons envelope. With each missile the range of Rmax and Rmin are different, as we discussed in Chapter 2. The fighter pilot must be aware of where he is in relation to his weapons envelope at all times in a fight. The gun is different from all of the missile types in that it has no minimum range. The gun weapons envelope is a 360-degree maximum-range circle around the bandit, with no minimum range.

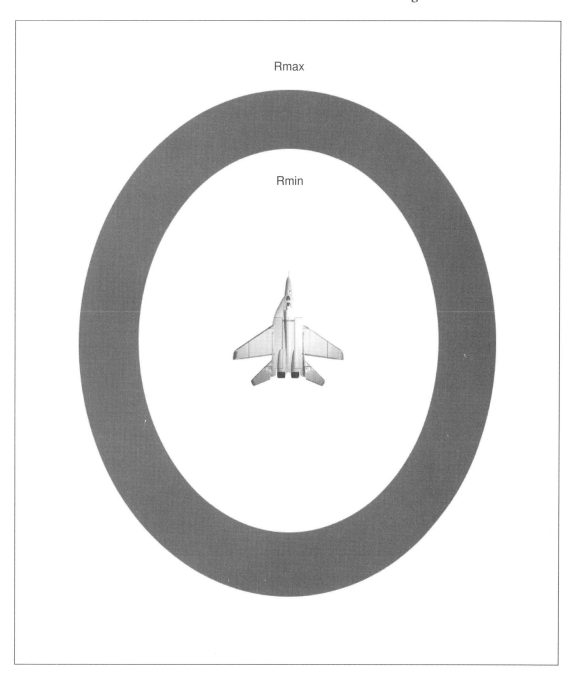

Figure 3-4. Weapons envelope

The Control Zone

The control zone, also called the *elbow*, is the location of the bandit's 6 o'clock, where you can establish a stable position in which to employ your weapons. From this location it is relatively easy to stay behind the bandit. This spot is called the elbow because when fighter pilots describe air combat with their hands, the elbow of the arm that is showing the bandit's motion is the approximate position of the control zone. In the JetFighter simulation, this position is about 2000 to 5000 feet behind the maneuvering bandit when the bandit is at corner velocity. Corner velocity is the speed at which an aircraft can make the fastest, tightest turn, and for the enemy aircraft in JetFighter this speed is approximately 450 knots. The control position gets closer to the bandit as it slows down. A 200-knot bandit, for example, has a control position of 1000 to 2500 feet. The reason for this is that at this slow speed the bandit cannot generate a very high turn rate, which allows you to get closer to him and still stay in control.

Figure 3-5. Control position

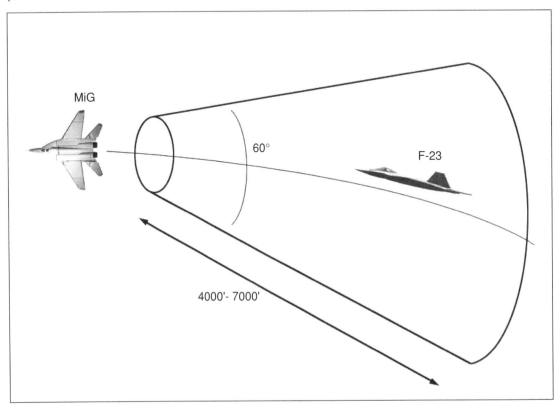

BFM is flown to arrive in the control position with 100 knots of overtaking airspeed (overtake), and within 30 degrees of the bandit's heading (angle-off). Figure 3-5 shows the JetFighter in the control position on the MiG.

All aircraft can execute only three very basic maneuvers. (All other maneuvers are simply combinations of these three basic maneuvers.) These maneuvers are roll, turn, and acceleration. Roll is used to position your lift vector. The nose of the aircraft will turn in the direction of the lift vector as you pull *G*s. Offensive BFM involves turning your jet to solve aspect, angle-off, and overtake problems that are caused by the bandit's turn. Unfortunately, this is no easy task. You must know precisely where and how to turn. To learn this, we'll discuss the characteristics of a turning jet.

THREE BASIC MANEUVERS

Turn Rate and Turn Radius

Every aircraft turn has measures, or parameters, that describe the turn. The two most important turn parameters for a fighter pilot to understand are *turn radius* and *turn rate*. Turn radius is a measure of how small a circle a jet is creating by turning. If you were looking down on the aircraft as it turned, the turn radius would be the distance from the center of the turn circle to the aircraft, measured in feet. Figure 3-6 shows this circle.

The equation for turn radius is:

TR (turn radius) = $V^2/g\,^G$

V is the aircraft's velocity in feet per second. Lowercase *g* is gravity and capital *G* is the *G* the aircraft is pulling.

It's not important that you understand how to compute turn radius, but it is important that you realize that V (velocity) is squared in the turn radius equation, which makes velocity the most important variable in the equation. You must control your aircraft velocity in order to minimize your turn radius because it's important, as you'll see later, to turn the aircraft with the smallest turn radius. The

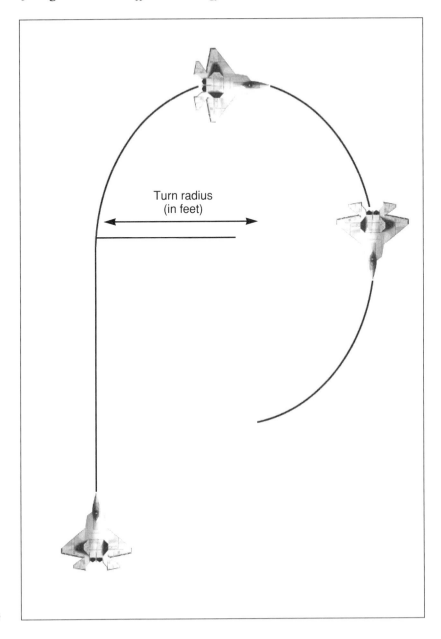

Figure 3-6. Turn circle

equation also includes aircraft *G*s. The more *G*s you pull, the tighter the turn.

Turn rate is the second important characteristic of turning the jet. The turn rate measures how fast the aircraft is moving around the turn circle we just discussed. Turn rate is measured in degrees per second, and is also dependent on *G*s and on airspeed.

Turn rate = K^G/V

K is a constant. Capital G and V are the same as they were in the equation for turn radius. This equation shows that you need to pull the maximum of Gs possible at the slowest airspeed (V) to get the highest turn rate. Turn rate is a measure of how fast you can put your nose on the bandit. Since you have to move the nose of your aircraft to shoot missiles or the gun at the bandit, a high turn rate is necessary in air-to-air combat.

In order to execute BFM in JetFighter (or in a real jet), you must be able to control your airspeed. In the JetFighter simulation, a good overall combat airspeed, once a turning fight is entered, is 400 to 500 knots. If you fly faster than this airspeed when you're trying to turn, you'll create a huge turn radius and a slow turn rate. Flying faster than 500 knots is not a good idea in a turning fight. If you fly slower than 400 knots your turn radius will be small but, again, your rate will go down because you'll be unable to achieve high Gs at a slow speed. If you're flying an air-to-air intercept and are going to turn and fight at endgame, you should enter the "merge" or the within-visual-range (WVR) fight, with your airspeed between 400 to 500 knots.

Acceleration

Acceleration measures how fast your airspeed increases. It is very important because BFM usually results in energy bleed-off and a fighter must be able to regain this energy by accelerating. In JetFighter II, when you're flying the F-23 you'll usually preserve your airspeed without too much trouble. If you find that you're slow, however, the best way to accelerate is to light the afterburner (AB), roll the wings level, and place your flight path marker below the horizon.

Up to this point, we've defined the needed BFM terms and equations. Now it's time to discuss specific JetFighter offensive BFM procedures. Before we start, I'd like to state up front that Within-Visual-Range maneuvering in a fighter simulation is limited due to several factors. The biggest challenge to fighting an enemy fighter in

**JETFIGHTER
OFFENSIVE
MANEUVERS**

the JetFighter simulation is the limited view of the combat arena provided by your computer monitor. This view is obviously more limited than my view from an F-16 cockpit. The other limit is the range at which you can make out details on the bandit that will tell you your range, aspect angle, and angle-off. In JetFighter (and in every other current PC-based simulation), the range where you can tell the position of the bandit is about 4000 feet. In a real fighter it's about 12,000 feet. This difference limits your reaction time in the simulation. Even with both of these limitation, however, you can still manage air-to-air combat. You just have to get close and react very quickly. This section will describe the procedures a fighter pilot must perform in order to master offensive maneuvering in the JetFighter simulation, along with some "workarounds" that will help you stay in an offensive position on the enemy fighter.

The Elbow

Offensive BFM is necessary because a bandit in fear of dying will turn his jet at high *G*s. The way to solve the BFM problems that are created by this turn is to execute a turn of your own with the objective of flying your jet to the elbow. The key to JetFighter II offensive BFM is knowing when and how to execute this turn. If you're behind a bandit, remember that the objective is to kill him, not to put on an air show at his 6 o'clock. The first step when you have a bad guy in or near your HUD is to shoot something at him. If you can't because the bandit starts a hard turn into you, then you must execute the following steps to get control of him and start shooting again:

1. Use the HUD and the HSD to *observe* the bandit. If you cannot determine the enemy's direction of turn by looking out of the HUD and seeing him, look at your HSD and you'll see the bandit moving right or left on the HSD. Be sure that you're on 4-mile range on the HSD. You can get to the 4-mile range scale by pressing [R] until you see the number 4 on the HSD.

2. When you observe the direction of turn for the bandit, *predict* his movement across the sky and start a turn in the same direction. For example, if the bandit moves to the left in your HUD or to the left on your HSD, turn left.

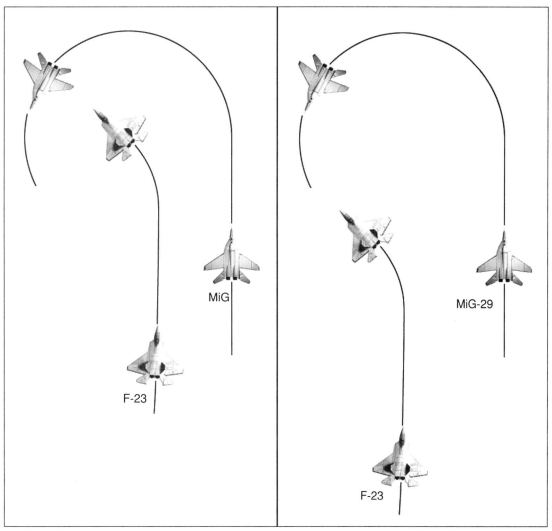

Figure 3-7. Attacking fighter inside and outside the turn circle

3. As you see that the bandit keeps turning out in front of you, ask yourself this question: "If the bandit keeps turning at his present rate, will his nose come around to point at me before I can close with him?" If the answer to this question is yes, then you are *outside* the MiG's turn circle and you're not flying offensive BFM—you're flying head-on BFM. You can't solve aspect, angle-off, and range problems when you're outside the bandit's turn circle. The reason for this is simple: no matter what you do, if you're outside the bandit's turn circle he can always point at you and force a head-on pass. Figure 3-7 shows a fighter both inside

and outside the turn circle. In JetFighter, when a bandit starts a defensive turn and you're outside his turn circle, he'll soon flash by you. We'll cover this head-on situation shortly, but for now let's assume we're inside the bandit's turn circle (the bandit's present turn rate will not bring his nose around to point at our jet).

4. Given that we're inside the turn circle, *maneuver* to place the flight path marker out in front of the bandit (lead pursuit) and start pulling 5 to 7 *G*s. Adjust the airspeed to gain 50 knots of closure (read the closure in the HUD).

5. You now must observe the movement of the bandit in your HUD to determine how you will *react*. The enemy fighter will do one of three things in relation to your flight path marker:

   • If the enemy fighter stays in the same spot in the HUD, your lead pursuit course is allowing you to match his turn rate. You should close the range and fly to the elbow. Stay in lead pursuit and prepare to shoot. If you're armed with Sidewinder missiles, shoot. If you're too close for a missile shot, switch to guns and fire when you're within 2000 feet. Figure 3-8 shows this gun firing position on the bandit.

   • If you pull the flight path marker to lead and the bandit moves under your nose, you're pulling too much lead. Ease off the *G* and let him fly back into the HUD field of view. Once he comes into view, put the flight path marker behind him in lag pursuit. Figure 3-9 shows a lag pursuit position on an enemy

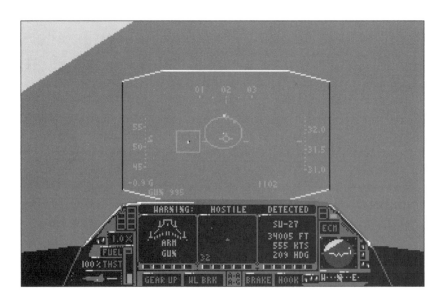

Figure 3-8. Gun attack position on a bandit

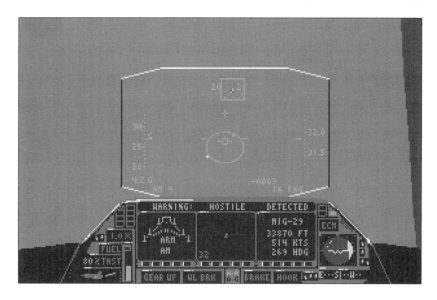

Figure 3-9. Lag pursuit on the bandit

fighter. As you get closer, the bandit will start moving away from you in the direction of the turn. When this occurs, go back to lead pursuit by putting your flight path marker in front of the bandit, and again get ready for a gun shot. In both of the above cases you may pass through Sidewinder parameters.

* If the bandit moves through the flight path marker and you go from lead to lag pursuit, you're not matching his turn rate.If this continues, you'll overshoot the bandit. An overshoot is when you fly past the bandit and go out in front of him. Figure 3-10 shows an overshoot. To avoid an overshoot, you should turn the jet as hard as possible and check your airspeed. If it's over 500 knots, you'll overshoot the bandit frequently (remember, velocity is squared in the rate and radius equations). If you do overshoot in JetFighter, not to worry. Just keep turning in the direction of the bandit and you'll get behind him.

These procedures are designed to get you to a control position on an enemy fighter. It's important that you carefully control your airspeed when flying offensive BFM. In the F-16 we have a saying, "Fight BFM with both hands." What this means is that you must not only move the stick but also the throttle when you are fighting. Failure to do so, both in the real jet and in the JetFighter II simulation, will

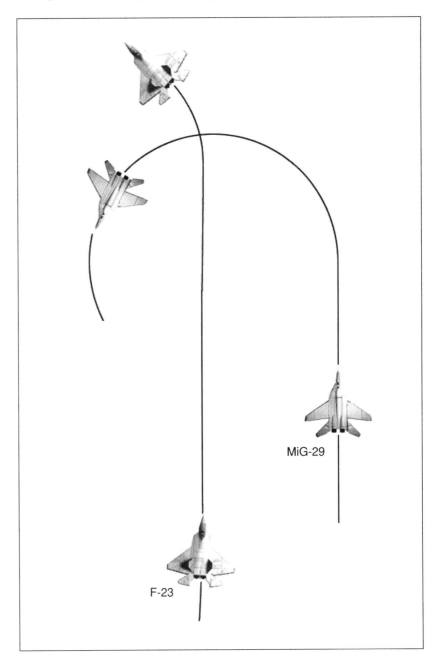

Figure 3-10. Overshoot

result in your riding those high-thrust engines right on past the bandit into a gross overshoot.

You can use the above procedures for maximizing "style points" while flying BFM in JetFighter II. If you're behind a bandit and get confused about what to do, remember these two points:

1. Always shoot when you're in range of your weapons.
2. If in doubt, turn in the shortest direction to bring the bandit to the nose, using the HUD or HSD.

The next section will cover what to do when you've cleverly trapped a bandit at your 6 o'clock.

JETFIGHTER DEFENSIVE MANEUVERS

Defensive BFM is very simple compared to offensive BFM. When flying defensively, all you really have to do is to create BFM problems for the bandit by turning at high *G*s until your lift vector is right on your attacker. The real key to defense is never to give up. Remember, when there's life there's hope.

Maneuvers and Countermeasures

You can tell from our previous discussion that offensive BFM is difficult to understand and execute in JetFighter. The key to defensive BFM is to take advantage of the difficulty of offensive BFM. In order to defend yourself, you simply give the bandit offensive BFM problems and then capitalize on his mistakes. In order to maximize the problems of an attacking bandit, execute the following defensive BFM procedures:

Missile Launch

You can detect a missile launch by using the JetFighter Communications Message panel. If you see or hear a missile launch indication at any time during a mission, you should immediately execute the following procedures:

1. Dispense chaff (strips of metal that appear on radar and are used as a decoy) and flares (pyrotechnic devices used to decoy infrared-guided missiles) and on turn your electronic countermeasures.

   Chaff: press Ⓒ
   Flares: press Ⓕ
   Electronic Countermeasures: press Ⓙ

   If you're sure of the missile type, then press only Ⓒ for a radar missile or Ⓕ for an IR- guided missile. If you're not sure, press both.

2. While you're using your chaff, flares, and electronic counter-measures, you must also put maximum *G*s on the jet at missile endgame. You can use the HSD to determine missile endgame by switching to the 4-mile range scale as the missile gets within 4 miles. When the missile is at 2 miles (or ¼ of the way down the scope), execute a break turn. Again, don't sweat which way to turn, just turn. A missile that is within 2 miles requires you to move quickly.

Bandit at 6 O'Clock

In the case where the bandit is at your 6 o'clock, look at the HSD to figure out the direction of your defensive turn and execute the following steps:

1. If the bandit is on the right side of the HSD, turn right. If he's on the left, turn left. If you can actually see the bandit by using a view out of the back of the jet, turn toward the bandit.

2. To execute this turn, roll to set your wings at approximately 80 to 90 degrees of bank and start a hard turn into the bandit at *maximum* G. Turn as hard as possible at the highest *G* available.

3. Next you must look at the HSD and note the direction of movement of the bandit on the screen.

   • If the bandit moves toward your nose, or 12 o'clock position, your turn is working. You're causing a problem the bandit can't solve, which will make him overshoot. Keep turning until he gets to your nose. At this point you're no longer on the defensive, but are now probably flying offensive or head-on BFM. Figure 3-11 shows a bird's-eye view of a successful defensive turn.

   • If you turn hard into the bandit and he doesn't move to the 12 o'clock position on the HSD, your defensive maneuver isn't working. Check your airspeed. This is always a good thing to do in any air-to-air situation when things aren't going well. If you're flying faster than 500 knots, slow down to give your jet a tighter turn circle. If you're slower than 400 knots and you're not in AB, get there by pressing the ⓪ twice. This should quickly restore your airspeed. Also, the bandit should start moving out in front of you. If he doesn't, just remember another important fighter axiom: "A MiG at 6 o'clock is better than no MiG at all."

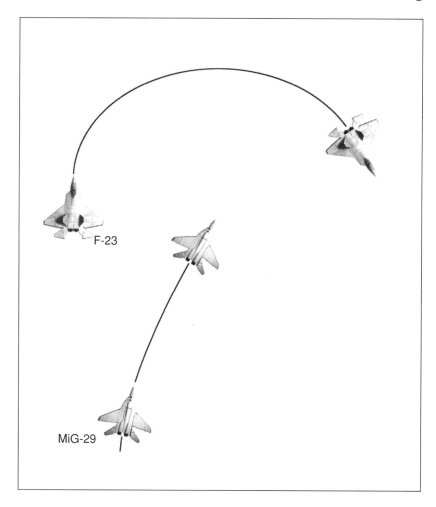

Figure 3-11.
Defensive turn

This BFM is flown after passing the bandit head-on. You have the option at this point to separate from the enemy by continuing on your present heading at maximum speed. You also have the option to turn and fight the bandit. If your mission is to kill him, then you have to know how to fight head-on BFM. JetFighter head-on BFM is very easy to perform if you follow these steps:

JETFIGHTER HEAD-ON MANEUVERS

1. Use the HSD and the HUD to point at the bandit (place him at your 12 o'clock position).

2. Whenever weapons parameters show in the HUD, shoot a Sidewinder or AMRAAM. If the missile doesn't work, switch to guns once you are inside of 1 mile.

3. Watch for weapons shot at your jet as you approach the bandit head-on. If you do get a launch indication on your Communication Message panel, execute the steps we discussed in the defensive BFM section. There should be no doubt in your mind: when somebody shoots at you, you're defensive even if he's not behind you.

4. When you "see" the bandit fly past you, either visually or on the HSD, start a hard turn at 7 or more *G*s in the direction of the bandit. Figure 3-12 shows a bird's-eye view of a head-on pass with

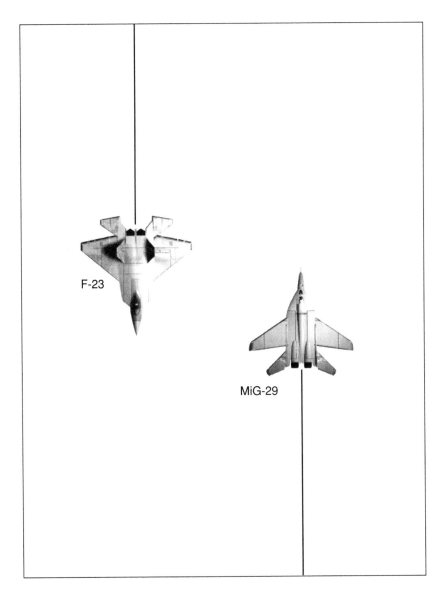

Figure 3-12. Head-on pass

the enemy fighter. If you're committed to fighting this bandit, then it's important that you initiate the turn quickly after passing him.

5. After starting a hard turn into the enemy fighter, you should keep the turn going until you get him in your HUD again. Once you start a head-on fight, you usually stay in it until you kill the bandit.

6. Any time you get really confused and that great big invisible hand reaches up from your computer and starts to choke you, remember this: always turn in the direction of the bandit. If you can't think of anything else to do, just keep turning into him, using the HSD as a reference.

One last point about head-on BFM: you can execute the hard turn into the bandit in the vertical as well as the horizontal plane. If you go into the vertical, just remember to keep on pulling all the way through until you're pointing at him again.

One-Circle and Two-Circle Fights

Another important concept for a fighter pilot to understand when flying head-on BFM is one-circle versus two-circle fights. When a bandit passes your jet head-on and starts to turn back toward your aircraft, you're faced with a decision as to which way to turn to get back around the enemy. Normally you'll turn in the same direction that the bandit passed in. In other words, if the bandit passed on your left side, you'd turn left to bring him to your nose. If the bandit was also turning left, this would create two-circle fight geometry, as shown in Figure 3-13. A two-circle fight is generally more desirable in JetFighter because it will give you more time to get a head-on missile shot.

If you're out of missiles, however, you should take the fight one-circle (also shown in Figure 3-13). This will jam the enemy fighter's head-on missile shot on your jet. To take the fight one-circle, you must determine which way the bandit is turning back into you and turn the opposite way. For example, in a head-on fight, if the bandit passes you on your left and turns left into you, you turn right to take the fight one-circle. Another time when you should take the fight one-circle is when you find yourself slow. In JetFighter, if you're down below 200 knots and are committed to a head-on fight, then

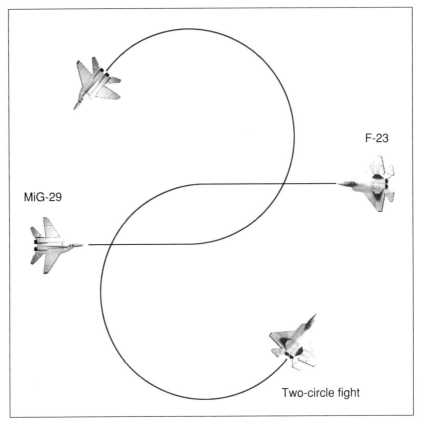

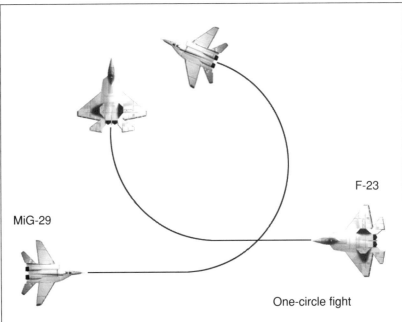

Figure 3-13. Two-circle fight and one-circle fight

take the fight one-circle. The reason for this is that your *turn radius* is very small, but your turn rate is poor at this airspeed. If you try to go two-circle, the bandit will get his nose around on you faster (because he has a higher turn rate) and will be pointing at you with a missile. If you go one-circle you might jam his missile.

We have discussed maneuvering from offensive, defensive, and head-on situations. The goal of all this is to survive the attack of the bandit and shoot him down.

Flying One versus One combat in an F-23 is a wonderful experience. Most One versus One maneuvering fights can be won easily by the F-23 due to its much higher sustained turn rate. When you are flying in the simulation and outmaneuvering an opponent, however, it's important to keep in mind that the real objective of the fight is to fill his cockpit with hair, teeth, and eyeballs as fast as possible. Arriving at 6 o'clock on the bandit is not the objective in an air-to-air fight— killing the bandit is. In order to do this, you have to shoot him with a missile or with the gun. For this reason, always think in terms of your weapons envelope and of ending the fight quickly with a missile or gun shot. Remember, in the JetFighter simulation (and in a real fight), you're never really one versus one. As you start to maneuver with one bandit, others will converge on the fight. Most guys get shot down by bandits who have entered the fight undetected. In order to minimize your exposure, kill quickly and get away from the fireball.

REMEMBER WHY YOU'RE THERE

ACT consists of engagements of more than two aircraft. All ACT is built on BFM tactics and on the bottom-line rule in ACT—*always fight your best One versus One tactics first before considering the effects of the other aircraft in the fight.* For example, if a decision is made to kill a bandit that's out in front of your jet, then you should fight your best One versus One offensive BFM to kill him, regardless of how many other bandits are in the area. The crucial part of this example (and the difficult part of any ACT engagement) is making the decision to engage and deciding how long the engagement will be. To kill a bandit that is out in front of your jet may be suicide if the air is filled with enemy jets and the engagement will require you to be

JETFIGHTER AIR COMBAT TACTICS (ACT)

anchored in a sustained turning fight. On the other hand, the decision to engage in offensive BFM may require that you turn for only a few degrees to get a kill. The point here is that ACT involves tactical decisions and that once these decisions are made, you execute sound BFM to carry them out.

This section will give you some actual fighter pilot rules of thumb to help you in JetFighter ACT engagements. Just keep in mind that ACT is just an extension of single-ship BFM.

One versus Many

Single-ship combat against multiple enemy aircraft is one of the most challenging air-to-air engagements that a fighter pilot will face. One versus Many tactics are challenging to execute, but are straightforward conceptually. We will divide our discussion of One versus Many tactics into offensive, defensive, and head-on scenarios. You are on the offensive in a One versus Many scenario if the bandits you're fighting are all out in front of your aircraft, as shown in Figure 3- 14. Staying on the offensive by keeping the bandits out in front is the difficult part of One versus Many offensive maneuvering. When

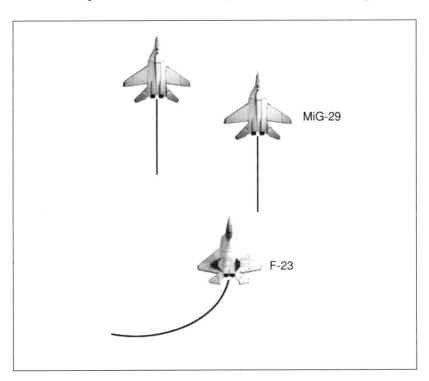

Figure 3-14. All bandits out in front of your jet

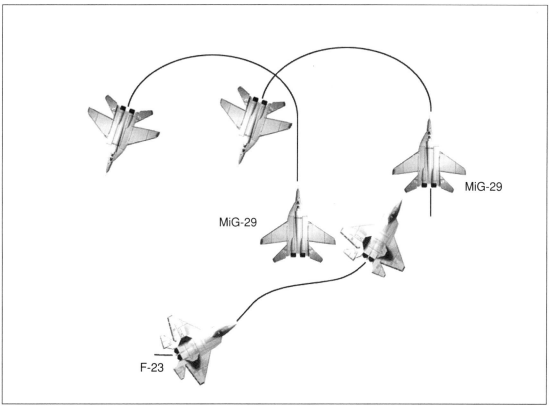

you enter a One versus Many fight in an offensive position, it's important that you *shoot* as *soon as possible at the nearest bandit, then maneuver to stay in control of the fight.* If you shoot a missile at the nearest bandit and hit him, then you've just improved the odds and changed the mindset of the surviving enemy fighters. If you miss your shot, the maneuvering is even more critical because you've just gotten them mad and they outnumber you.

A rule of thumb for maintaining control of the fight when you're a single aircraft fighting multiple bandits is to *try to keep the bandits on one side of your jet.* In other words, maneuver so that when you look out of the cockpit you see all of the enemy aircraft on the same side. This will make it much easier to keep the bandits in sight and will make it harder for them to sandwich you. Figure 3-15 illustrates how this works when you're fighting two bandits. In addition to keeping them on one side of your jet, you should also *try to keep all of the bandits either above or below you in altitude.* Again this will make it easier to keep track of the bandits and keep you from getting trapped.

The question may come up: "What do I do if there are more than two bandits in a fight and I don't kill one before they see me and start a turning engagement?" The answer is simple—separate from the fight. A rule of thumb is that if you're alone and there are more than two bandits, *do not turn more than 90 degrees to get a shot or let your airspeed bleed off below 400 knots.* After reaching 90 degrees of turn or coming down to 400 knots, get out of the fight. The way to separate from the fight is to pass the bandits as close as possible at 180 degrees of heading crossing angle at the "speed of heat." Figure 3-16 depicts a successful separation. Separating from fights is an art more than a science, and it's a critical fighter pilot skill.

A defensive One versus Many fight starts when a bandit gets

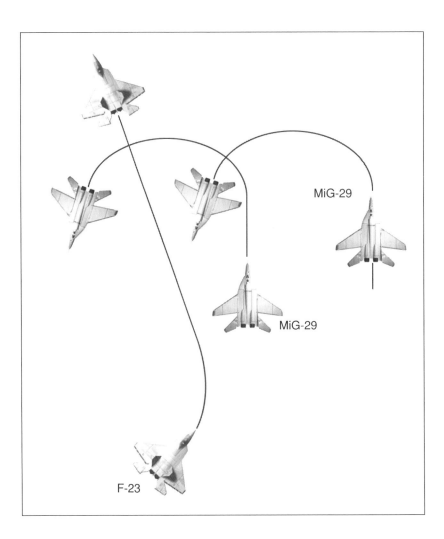

Figure 3-16.
Separating from the fight

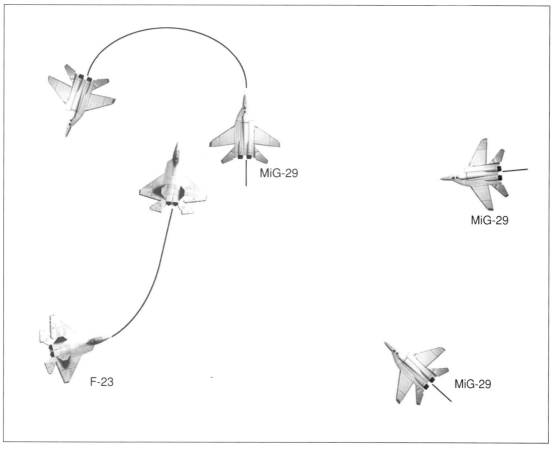

MiG-29

MiG-29

MiG-29

F-23

Figure 3-17.
Defensive turn against
the most immediate
threat

behind your 3 o'clock/9 o'clock line with nose position (his nose is with 45 degrees of your aircraft). Remember that bad things can happen to you when the bandit puts his nose on you within range of his weapons. When this occurs, you should fight your best One versus One defensive BFM, which we've already discussed. It makes no difference how many bandits are in the sky around you. The rule of thumb on the defense is to *fight One versus One BFM against the most immediate threat.* Figure 3-17 shows what I mean. When you've defeated this attack, you'll probably have another bad guy saddling up on you, so get ready to continue to fight the next guy who engages you. When you're fighting multiple bandits, remember that one guy may come off you to give another guy who is in a better position a chance to kill you. *If you see one bandit disengaging, keep checking 6 (6 o'clock) because you're about to be engaged by his wingmen.* If this does not occur, keep accelerating and leave the area.

A head-on One versus Many fight is a very simple scenario. If you pass multiple bandits head-on, plug in the Afterburner and don't turn, just keep right on going. It is very foolhardy to start a One versus Many fight from a head-on pass. In fact, the only way you should initiate a One versus Many fight is from an offensive position. In any other scenario, the goal is to get out of the fight as quickly as possible.

Two versus Many

Two versus Many fights are conceptually very similar to One versus Many engagements (which are an extension of One versus One BFM). The difference in a Two versus Many fight is that your wingman can even up the odds and give you several additional options that you don't have as a single ship. The presence of a wingman, however, does not mean that you abandon the principles of One versus Many air combat or fight any differently. Keep in mind that your wingman may blow up at just the wrong time, or get engaged by a surface-to-air missile and leave you in a bad position. For this reason always fight your best One versus One BFM and follow the One versus Many rules of thumb that we've discussed. The biggest difference between One versus Many and Two versus Many fights is that you can stay in a turning fight longer to achieve a kill if you have a wingman. This does not mean that you can disregard your "escape window" (discussed below).

The presence of a wingman does mean, however, that you can delay a separation and spend more energy in the form of airspeed and altitude in the fight, because your wingman can pick off any other bandits that try to enter the fight. In addition, if you start to get too slow, your wingman can enter the fight and you can extend and get your energy back. Remember, in Two versus Many fights your wingman will probably become engaged soon after the merge and you'll suddenly be thrust into a One versus Many fight.

Separating From a Fight

In all air-to-air fights, the fighter pilot must be aware of his escape window. You can think of the escape window as your safe path out of an aerial engagement. When you're undetected by the enemy, your escape window is the size of a hangar and you can easily fly through it and disengage at any time. When the bandit detects your jet, however, your escape window closes down. When multiple bandits in JetFighter II start to maneuver at close range against your jet, the escape window starts to shrink.

The best way to keep an escape window open in JetFighter is to kill whenever you get in a weapons envelope on the enemy and keep your smash (speed) up. Avoid long turning engagements, and after one 360-degree turn with an enemy fighter, extend out of the fight. To extend out of the fight, pass the most threatening bandit at high angle-off, put your nose below the horizon, and accelerate as fast as possible in Afterburner. Figure 3-18 shows an example of a successful engagement and separation.

Figure 3-18.
Successful attack and separation

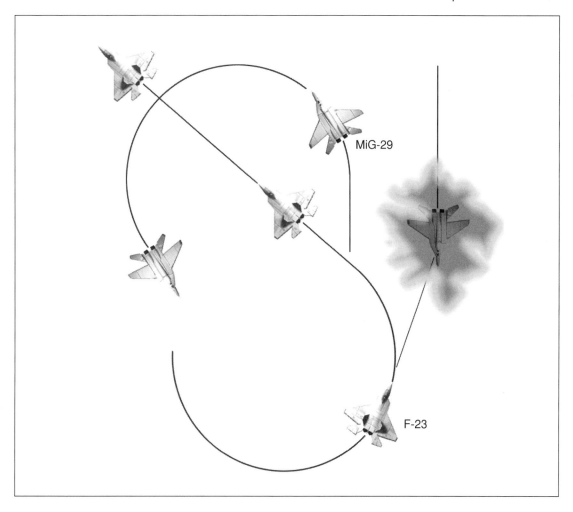

As you execute your separation, monitor your HSD to ensure that you are in fact pulling away from the enemy. Give it some time, but if the bad guys are staying with you and are still shooting, your escape window is closed. The only way to reopen it is to turn and kill someone. Besides, any bandit with the audacity to try to run down an F-23 deserves a missile anyway.

The biggest mistake in JetFighter II (and in most real air-to-air engagements) is staying too long in an anchored turning fight. If you don't get a quick kill, you should think about extending out of the fight and then either heading for home or re-engaging from beyond visual range (BVR) using your stealthy aircraft.

JETFIGHTER II TACTICAL INTERCEPTS

The strength of the F-23 in JetFighter II is that it combines high maneuverability and excellent air-to-air weapons with an LO (Low Observable) airframe. In JetFighter II the best way to take advantage of these features is to maneuver for a position of advantage when you are still BVR on the bandits. This is called doing an intercept.

We will discuss two basic types of intercepts that work in JetFighter II and take advantage of your aircraft weapons and LO characteristics. The first of these we'll call a *min time to ram* intercept. We will use this intercept when we have to close on the target in a big hurry and get a shot. Several JetFighter missions start with Cruise missiles inbound to the city. On these missions you must close quickly with the targets and destroy them. This intercept will work for these and othertime-critical situations. The other intercept we will discuss is the *stern conversion*. This intercept is used when you have more time. It places you behind the bandit for a tail shot, but it takes longer to complete than the min time to ram intercept.

Min Time to Ram Intercept

This intercept is designed to put you in a position for a flank shot on target in minimum time. Figure 3-19 shows a god's-eye view of this intercept, along with some defined positions around the target used by fighter pilots during intercepts. The basic positions are nose, flank, beam, and tail, as shown in Figure 2-4.

Up to this point, we have not discussed the use of the Map view in JetFighter air-to-air combat. I prefer not to use the Map view in a close-in maneuvering fight, but before you get within 4 miles of the

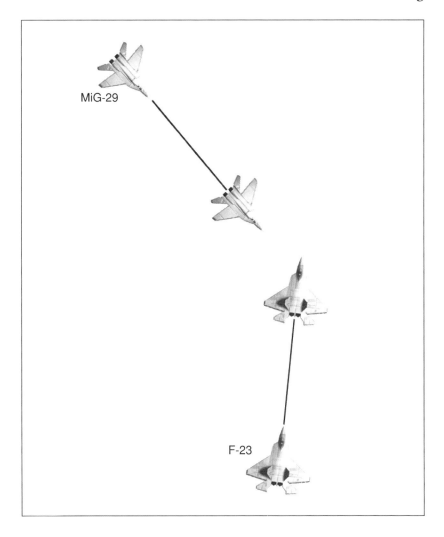

Figure 3-19. Min time to ram intercept

bandit, the Map view is very useful. Here's how you do it. Early in a sortie, you should call up the Map view to build your situation awareness of the air combat arena. When enemy fighters are detected using the Map view, you must decide whether you're going to engage them or not. The factors affecting this decision will be discussed later in the book; for now, let's assume that you're going to engage the enemy. Further, let's assume that you need to get to the target in a hurry. Here are the steps you need to take to execute a min time to ram intercept.

1. Look at the Map view and predict the target's movements through the sky based on his present nose position as seen on the Map display.

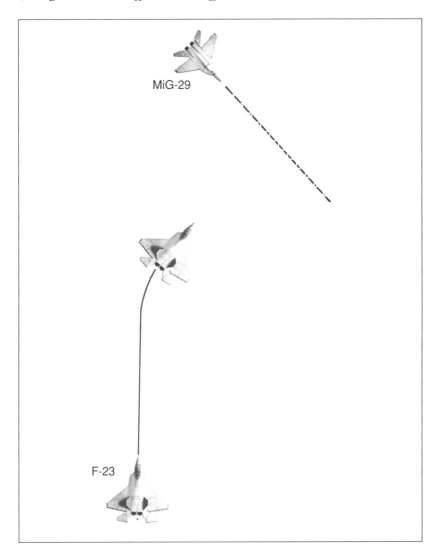

Figure 3-20. Turn to a heading to cross bandit's flight path

2. Figure a heading for your jet in order to cross the target's flight path. Exit the Map view by pressing $\boxed{M}$, return to the cockpit view, and turn the jet to this heading. Figure 3-20 shows how to accomplish this step.

3. As the target gets closer, keep changing the HSD range scale, using the $\boxed{R}$ key to keep the target at the top of the screen. In other words, if the target is in the bottom third of your screen on any range scale other than the 4-mile scale (you can't get any lower than 4-mile scale), then reduce the range scale. This technique, by the way, is a common fighter pilot procedure when doing intercepts.

4. Once you're established on this heading, push it up to full AB if you're not already there, and keep driving in. When the target gets to 7 miles, or about halfway down the HSD on the 15-mile range setting, analyze the geometry by switching to the Map view.

   If you have a flank, beam, or tail aspect on the target, throttle back to 80 percent to control your overtake. Keep closing and when you're in parameters—shoot.

   If you have nose aspect on the target, then check turn away 45 to 60 degrees for 5 seconds and retard the throttle to 80 percent. After 5 seconds, turn back into the target and shoot when you're in range.

5. After shooting a missile, check turn slightly away from the target and prepare for a reattack. If the missile shreds the target, move on to your next target. If the missile fails to guide, turn back into the target and shoot again.

This intercept is designed to get you to the target in minimum time for a flank shot. A flank shot will allow you to get around behind the bandit for another shot if you miss, and will still get you into weapons parameters in minimum time. A tail or beam shot is even better for a re-attack, but it takes longer to drive around to the beam or tail of the bandit. A head-on shot is obviously the fastest way to get a shot on the bandit, but a re-attack is very difficult and time-consuming.

Stern Conversion

A stern conversion places you at tail aspect on the bandit. This is the best intercept to fly if you have the time to complete it. A stern conversion takes advantage of your LO features and will usually place you undetected at the bandit's 6 o'clock. From this tail aspect position, you can take multiple shots at the enemy from a stabilized position. Here is how you fly a stern conversion in JetFighter II:

1. Call up the Map view by pressing ⓜ. Once you have the Map view up, note the target's position and heading. Point at the target using the Map view, then go back to the cockpit view by pressing ⓜ again.

2. Ensure that your HSD is on the 32-mile setting and see if the

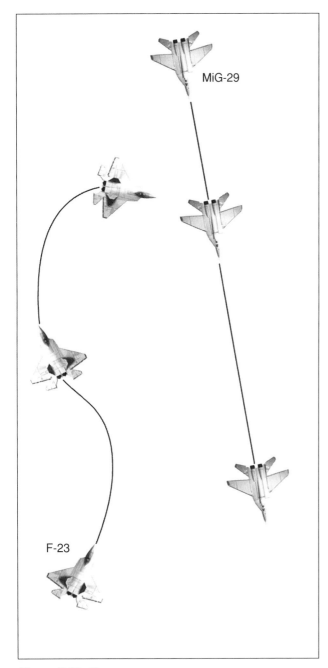

Figure 3-21. Turn away from the bandit to get lateral displacement

targets appear. If they do not appear, and you're pointing at them, keep pressing in until they do appear. Once the targets get within 32 miles, go back to the Map view and analyze the geometry.

3. If the target aspect is beam or tail, go to AB and run the bandits down. All you need to do in this case is to close the range and shoot. If the aspect is flank or nose, turn 45 to 60 degrees away from the bandit to get lateral displacement. When you do this turn for displacement, do not cross an imaginary line that extends straight out the bandit's nose This will ensure that you get the maximum displacement in the minimum time. Figure 3-21 shows how to execute this maneuver.

4. After executing your turn for displacement, switch back to the Map view to check the geometry. If the bandit detects your presence he'll turn into you. Watch for that, using the Map view. If it happens, turn immediately to put the bandit on the nose and get ready to duke it out head-to-head. If the bandit is still on the same course he was on at the start of the intercept, then he has not detected that he is about to die nice and relaxed (since he doesn't even know that he's under attack).

5. To complete the intercept, note when you are abeam the bandit, as shown in Figure 3-22. When this occurs, put the bandit on the nose and go full AB to close the range.

6. When you are within 4 miles of the target, slow to match the bandit's airspeed. Remember that the airspeed of the target that you are locked to can be read in the right MFD. Close to between 1 and 2 miles from the target. From here, you can shoot from a stabilized position.

Once you start blowing up the bad guys, it will dawn on them that somebody is in their chili. At this time you'll be in for a maneuvering fight.

This concludes our discussion of air-to-air combat. In the next chapter we will discuss the Sport of Kings (also known as blowing things up on the ground).

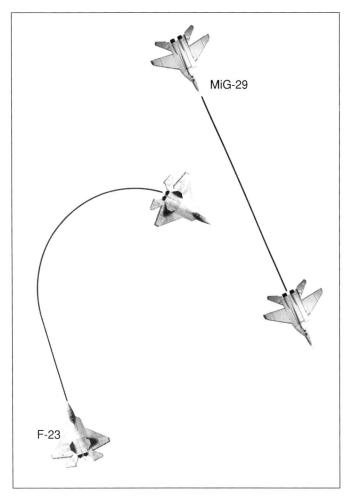

Figure 3-22. Turn to put the bandit on the nose

4 **Air-to-Ground Attack Tactics**

One of the serious problems in planning against American doctrine is that the Americans do not read their manuals, nor do they feel any obligations to follow their manuals.
—*Soviet officer*

Attacking targets on the ground is a big challenge in JetFighter II. JetFighter has guided air-to-air missiles for enemy fighters and many other advanced systems for navigation and self-defense, but when it comes to destroying a target attached to Mother Earth, the jet is very primitive. I found the air-to-ground part of the JetFighter II simulation to be very refreshing, because I grew up in the F-4 Phantom. The old Rhino (the pilot's name for the F-4) didn't have a dependable computer air-to-ground delivery system, so we had to bomb manually. Manual bombing is a Zen-like activity that requires the pilot to "become one with the bomb." You have to learn to "think like a bomb" in order to be a good manual bomber. JetFighter II requires the pilot to bomb manually because there are no fancy precision guided air-to-ground weapons in the simulation.

I learned manual bombing the same way you're going to have to learn it. First I received some basic academic theory on manual bombing, then I went out and dove at the ground a couple of thousand times until I became one with the bomb. This chapter will give you the academic theory, and then it's up to you to take the jet out over enemy territory and fill the sky with Mark-82s and Mark-84s. This is one part of the JetFighter II simulation that will give you a very good idea of what it's like to drop bombs from a real jet.

Along with bombs, JetFighter II has two other weapons that can be used to destroy ground targets. These weapons are the 20-mm cannon and the AIM-166 KEM. These two weapons can be treated the same for air-to-ground use. The AIM-166 is a high velocity rocket, but it is employed against ground targets in JetFighter II in almost exactly the same way as the 20-mm cannon. The gun and the KEM are "point-and-shoot" weapons, and they're easier to use than bombs for obvious reasons (you guessed it, you just point at the target and shoot). Later in this chapter we'll discuss a few techniques that will help you to hit the target more consistently and rack up style points along the way.

BOMBING   Before we start diving at the ground and dropping bombs, we first need to briefly discuss the mechanics of bombing. The free-fall bomb has been, and still is, the primary air-to-ground weapon used by fighters throughout the world. There's nothing fancy about a free-fall bomb. Modern fighters usually carry onboard computers that assist the pilot in aiming dumb bombs at the target. JetFighter doesn't have a computer system for helping you hit the target with your dumb bombs, but not to worry. By the end of this chapter you'll be a skilled manual bomber who scoffs at silicon-chip-aided bomb deliveries, because you'll be well on your way to becoming one with the bomb.

The Bombing Triangle

Figure 4-1 shows a side view of the bombing triangle. This triangle displays the mechanics of a free-fall bomb. There are a few terms that the pilot must know in order to understand the geometry of manual bombing:

Flight Path Marker: the marker displayed in the pilot's HUD that shows the path of the aircraft through the sky. If the pilot were to continue to dive at the ground until impact, the aircraft would hit the ground exactly on the flight path marker.

Figure 4-1. Bombing triangle

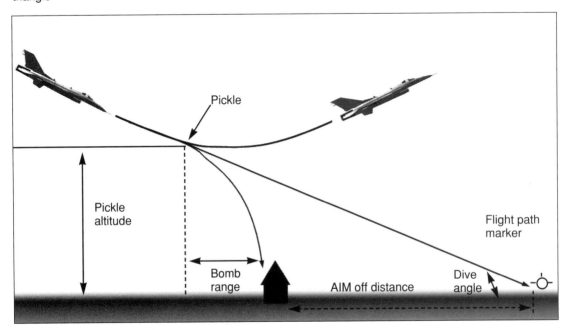

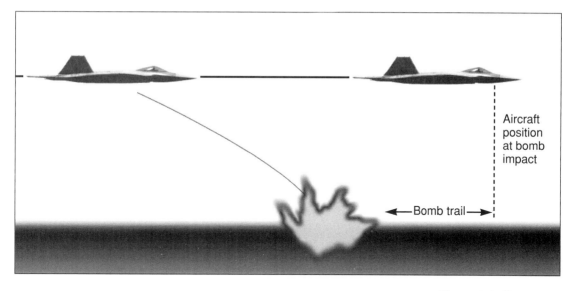

Figure 4-2. Bomb trail

Aim Off Distance: the distance, measured in feet, from the flight path marker to the target.

Bomb Range: the horizontal distance, measured in feet, from the aircraft to the target at bomb release.

Dive Angle: the angle, measured in degrees, between the flight path of the jet and the horizon.

Pickle Altitude: the height of the aircraft above the ground, in feet, at bomb release.

Figure 4-2 shows another important manual bombing concept— bomb trail.

Bomb Trail: the distance, measured in feet, from the bomb impact to the delivery aircraft.

When an aircraft drops a bomb it "trails" behind the aircraft because it is unpowered, while the aircraft, of course, is being pushed by its engines. For this reason a bomb will not fall beyond the flight path marker. In other words, if you are diving at a target and put the flight path marker short of the target, then you'll always get a short bomb. There is no way for the bomb to go farther than the spot where your jet is pointing, because the bomb has the greatest speed right at the point of release. The bomb takes the aircraft vector at release; after that, gravity and friction take over and it's literally downhill from there on.

The exception to this occurs if you pulse the stick. In the case of a very sudden input to the flight controls, you're not really changing the flight path of the aircraft (even though the position of the flight path marker in the HUD may change). In this case, the bomb may fly just about anywhere. I'm sure there are a few guys with thick glasses that could figure out where the bomb will end up, but the pilot in the jet will have no idea. I've dropped a few bombs this way, and I didn't even see where some of them landed. The others I wished I hadn't seen, because they landed a long way from where I was aiming. The bottom line is that you must fly the aircraft smoothly when dropping bombs, or standard Newtonian physics (which is almost understandable to the fighter pilot) will be replaced by quantum mechanics or something else equally strange, and you will have no idea where the bomb will go.

Now that we've defined the terms, it's time to dive right into a discussion of bombing techniques in JetFighter II. There are two different types of bombing passes that we will discuss. The first is a level bomb pass and the second is a dive bomb pass.

Level Bomb

A level bomb is used when you want to stay close to the ground to avoid the threat of enemy fire. It is the easiest bombing attack to execute in JetFighter II because you get right down amongst them and fill the HUD with the target. Here is how you drop a level bomb in JetFighter II:

1. **Select the weapon.** There are two types of bombs in JetFighter II, the Mark-82 500-pounder and the Mark-84 2000-pound bomb. Both of these bombs can be used for just about any target in the simulation, but I usually start out by dropping the smaller Mark-82 because you normally have more of them on the jet. To call up the desired weapon, press F1 until the stores management panel appears on the left MMD. Figure 4-3 shows a F-23 with the Mark-82 selected. You'll immediately notice in Figure 4-3 that there is no aiming symbology that pops up in the HUD. The only HUD aiming cues that you have for bombing in JetFighter II are the flight path marker and a TD box that will be laid over the target. With skill and cunning, these cues will be enough.

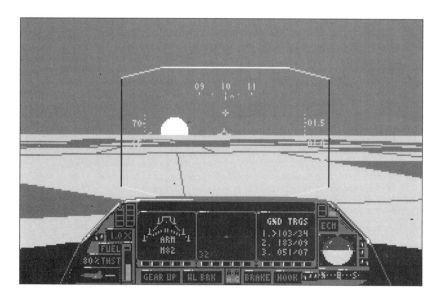

Figure 4-3. F-23 cockpit with Mark-82 selected

2. **Call up steering to the target.** To do this, press F2 until "GND TRGS" (ground targets) appears on the right MFD. Another way to call up this display is to simply press F7. The ground targets display, also shown in Figure 4-3, will provide the pilot with a list of numbered targets along with a mark to show which target is selected. The pilot can move this mark—in other words, select a new target—by pressing T. When you first enter this screen, the mark will always come up on target number 1. Also, for bombing missions, the screen will always appear when you enter the cockpit, but no target will be selected. The only way that you can select a target is to call up a weapon in the left MMD.

It is important to note that calling up the "GND TRGS" only provides steering to a selected target. Selecting a target does not in any way affect the bombing solution. All it does is give you a steering cue to the target in the HUD and a TD box over the target when you get within 10 miles of the target. In other words, if you're flying toward one target that is selected in the right MFD and you see another one and decide to bomb it, you don't need to select this new target in order to hit it. If you would like a TD box over the new target and a HUD steering cue, you have to press T to call up the new target. If it's not on the target list in the right MFD, you can't select it but you can still bomb it. Also, you can't select a target if you don't have a Mark-82 or Mark-84 called up on the left MMD. You'll still get a heading to fly, which is displayed on the GND TRGS screen, but you won't get a HUD steering cue or a TD box until you select a bomb.

3. **After calling up the proper steering displays, follow them to the target.** To do this, line up the steering cue directly in the center of the HUD, as shown in Figure 4-4. By following this steering cue you'll fly directly to the target selected on the right MFD in the GND TRGS display.

4. **When you're first learning to bomb, start the attack at 20 miles from the target.** To execute this attack, start a descent that will put you at or below 20,000 feet at 20 miles from the target. Continue your descent as you approach the target in order to level off at 2000 feet before reaching 10 miles out. At the 10-mile point, power back to 70 percent by pressing ⑦. Remember, you get the range to the selected target in the right MFD.

5. **As you approach 5 miles, start a gentle descent down to 1000 feet by placing the flight path marker right over the target (which is under the TD box in the HUD).** This will keep you lined up on the target and get you down to the proper altitude for the level bomb pass. At 5 miles, press ⑥ to reduce the power to 60 percent.

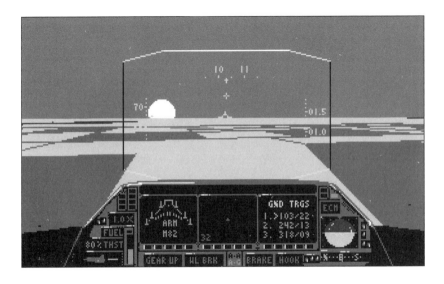

Figure 4-4. Steering cue centered in the HUD

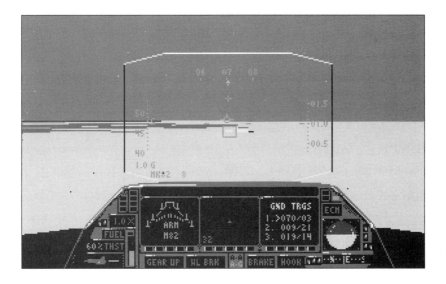

Figure 4-5. Level flight with the flight path marker on the horizon

6. **When you reach 1000 feet, level off by placing the flight path marker right on the horizon.** Figure 4-5 shows this position.

7. **Keep driving in at the target.** When the target tracks down toward your cockpit and is just about to pass under your nose— PICKLE! You pickle, or drop, the bomb by pressing [Spacebar] or the #1 button on your joystick. After pickling off the bomb, press [F9] to ride the bomb toward the target. This will give you immediate feedback on how your level bomb delivery went.

8. **Once you destroy the target, press [T] to select another target and follow your steering to set up another pass.**
   If you missed the target you may want to re-attack. "Re-attack" is a dreaded word to a fighter pilot, because it's very dangerous to drop bombs near someone and miss. It's even more dangerous to miss and then come back and try it again. In JetFighter II, re-attacks are usually safe to execute, but you must be aware of the tactical situation before committing to a re-attack. To re-attack from a level pass, keep driving straight away from the target until you reach the 6-mile point. At this point, make a level turn to line up with the target again and repeat the attack. As you execute your re-attack, you should do what fighter pilots call error analysis. In other words, try to figure out why the bomb missed and correct your mistake. Here are a few basic rules of thumb to help you out.

BOMBING PARAMETERS FOR JETFIGHTER II LEVEL BOMB

Dive Angle	0 degrees
Release Altitude	1000 feet
Release Airspeed	400 to 450 knots
Release Point	Target just approaching the cockpit

Dive angle errors: If you're climbing and release with the correct sight picture, the bomb will go long. If you are diving, it will go short.

Release altitude errors: Level bomb passes in JetFighter II are somewhat insensitive to small altitude deviations. This is because your sight picture changes and you release the bomb at a different slant range, which compensates for your altitude error. In other words, if you are high, for example, the sight picture of the target passing under the nose will occur sooner and you will release the bomb farther away from the target. This will make up for the longer bomb range caused by flying a higher altitude.

Release airspeed errors: If you are outside the proper release airspeed window, the bomb will go long if you are fast and short if you are slow.

Release sight picture errors: These errors are the most critical. During a level bomb pass you're traveling across the ground at about 850 feet per second. You can calculate your no-wind ground speed in feet per second by multiplying your airspeed by 1.69. What this means is that aiming errors are your biggest concern. If you delay your pickle by just half a second, you'll have a 425-foot miss. That is why you must develop your own aiming and pickling techniques. In the level bomb pass just described, I gave you my release sight

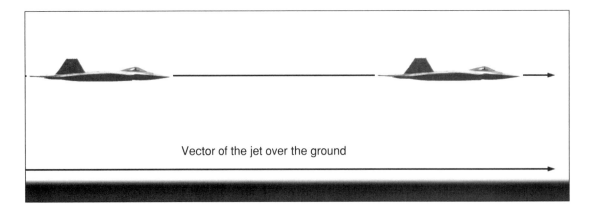

Vector of the jet over the ground

picture. If this one doesn't work for you, you'll have to do a little error analysis to come up with your own.

Dive Bomb

The dive bomb delivery is used when the tactical situation dictates that you stay high. We will discuss tactical mission planning in detail in Chapter 6. A dive bomb delivery is a very difficult attack to execute in JetFighter II or in a real jet. The reason that targets are hard to hit with a dive bomb attack can be summed up in two words—slant range. You're farther away from the target (at a greater slant range), so all of your aiming errors are multiplied. Diving at the target improves your chances of hitting it when you're at medium

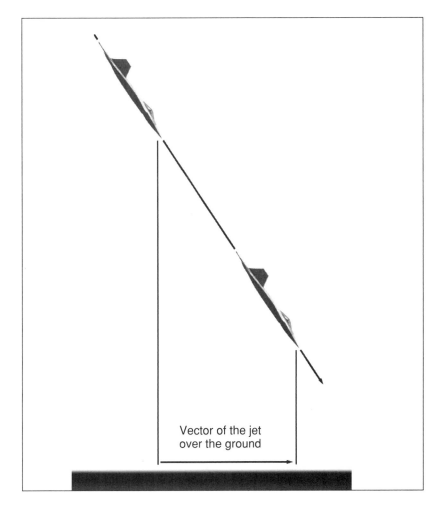

Vector of the jet
over the ground

Figure 4-6. Effect of dive on ground speed

altitude, because in a dive the jet is not tracking over the ground as fast as it is in a level bomb delivery. This gives you a better chance to pickle the bomb off at the proper sight picture. Figure 4-6 illustrates the effect of a dive on ground speed.

1. **Select the weapon.** Remember, you do this with the [Enter] key. Just keep pressing [Enter] until a Mark-82 or Mark-84 appears in the left MMD.

2. **Call up steering to the target.**

Steering to the target is selected by pressing [F7] . This will give you the GND TRGS display in the right MFD. Another way to get to GND TRGS is to keep pressing [F2] until "GND TRGS" appears in the right MFD. You will now get a steering cue on the HUD heading scale and a TD box over the target when the range to the target is 10 miles or less.

3. **After calling up the correct steering display, fly directly to the target.**

4. **When you're 20 miles out from the target, start a climb or descent to place your jet at 10,000 feet in level flight.** When you reach 10,000 feet, set the power at 60 percent by pressing [6] .

5. **Keep driving in at the target.** Figure 4-7 shows a dive bomb

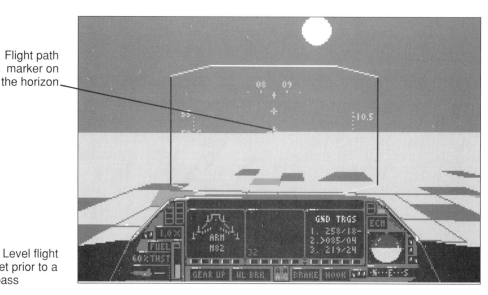

Flight path
marker on
the horizon

Figure 4-7. Level flight at 10,000 feet prior to a dive bomb pass

Figure 4-8. Dive bomb pass

delivery with your jet in level flight at 10,000 feet just before roll-in. When you reach 3 miles from the target, start a roll-in by pushing straight forward on the stick until the TD box appears in the HUD. Place the flight path marker just above the TD box, as shown in Figure 4-8.

6. **When you reach 7000–6800 feet—pickle!** This will happen very fast if you have a lazy roll-in at the start of the attack. It is important that you push the stick aggressively forward when you reach 3 miles, in order to give the jet time to stabilize with the flight path marker just above the target.

7. **After pickling off the bomb, start a wings level pull straight up toward the horizon.** As you approach the horizon, ease off the *G* and press `F9` to monitor the bomb impact.

This is not an easy attack to execute. You will have to practice this one and develop your own techniques, because the longer slant range to the target makes bombing from this altitude very difficult. You'll find that developing proficiency in dive bombing will be well worth the time it takes in the JetFighter II simulation. The dive bomb delivery gives you a medium-altitude air-to-ground attack option that will come in handy when you're attacking a target where a low-altitude approach is too dangerous.

STRAFING AND ROCKET ATTACKS

The JetFighter 20-mm cannon and the AIM-166 KEM are primarily air-to-air weapons, but both can be used against "soft" ground targets. It is important to note that in JetFighter II the only targets that you can shoot on the ground with the 20-mm or the KEM are parked aircraft. The JetFighter II software will only allow the gun and the KEM to destroy aircraft (either in the air or on the ground). So in this section, when we discuss attacking ground targets using the gun or KEM, we're talking about attacking only aircraft on the ground.

Strafing is shooting at targets on the ground with the gun. A rocket attack is very similar to a strafe pass in JetFighter II (or in a real fighter), so we will discuss only one attack technique for both of these "point-and-shoot" weapons.

1. **Select the weapon.** The weapon you select, however, may surprise you. Select a Mark-84. When you select a bomb (a Mark-84 or Mark-82), you'll get HUD steering to the target. This steering will come in the form of a heading cue and a TD box. With the TD box in the HUD, it's very difficult to find the targets. The reason that you will not get a TD box in the HUD when you select the gun or the KEM is that these are both primarily air-to-air weapons. The TD box display is reserved for airborne enemy aircraft when you have the gun or the AIM-166 KEM selected. That's why we start our strafe or rocket attack with a bomb selected. If we don't get a TD box in the HUD to help us find the target, we'll be stuck doing the old "Helen Keller routine," groping around trying to find the target.

2. **Press** F7 **to call up the GND TRGS display on the right MFD.**

3. **You can fly your strafe attack from any profile, but I prefer a run at the target that starts from 5000 feet, 4 miles out.** You can get on this "wire" (or attack profile) by approaching the target at 5000 feet and pushing over to pick up the HUD TD box when you get to the 4-mile point. Retard the throttle to 50 percent by hitting 5, and be sure that your flight path marker is below the target.

Figure 4-9 shows the F-23 on the wire for a KEM rocket attack. We initially placed the flight path marker directly below the target to produce a smooth and controlled approach. As we approach the target, we'll only have to bring the aiming reticle up to the target,

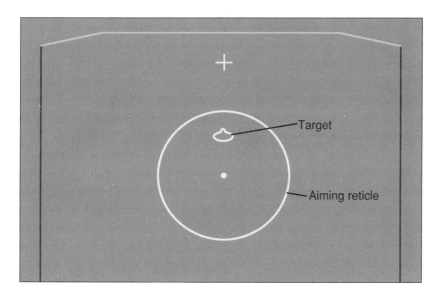

Figure 4-9. Lined up for a rocket pass

rather than solve the 6 o'clock/12 o'clock aiming problem. If you let your flight path marker wander as you roll in on the target, you may have 6/12 aiming problems as well as 3 o'clock/9 o'clock errors. You can usually handle errors in one direction, but not in both.

4. **After acquiring the target, under the HUD TD box press** ⌷Enter⌷ **twice to get to the Gun mode, or three times to select KEM, depending on which weapon you want to hose off.** The TD box will disappear as soon as you deselect Mark-82 or Mark-84.

5. **The aiming reticle should be below the target, as shown in Figure 4-9.** Gradually move the reticle up to the target and open fire when the top of the reticle touches the target. When the pipper (the small aiming dot in the center of the reticle) reaches the target, hold in there and keep firing. If you are firing KEM, shoot five to ten missiles per pass. If you are shooting the gun, fire five short bursts as you dive at the target.

Common Strafe and Rocket Pass Errors

When making a strafe or rocket pass, be careful not to use too much bank if you have a small azimuth (3 o'clock/9 o'clock) correction to make. Remember, bank angle causes the jet to turn. Your aiming reticle is not on the roll axis of the aircraft, so when you turn you'll create a pendulum effect. Figure 4-10 shows this effect. Small bank

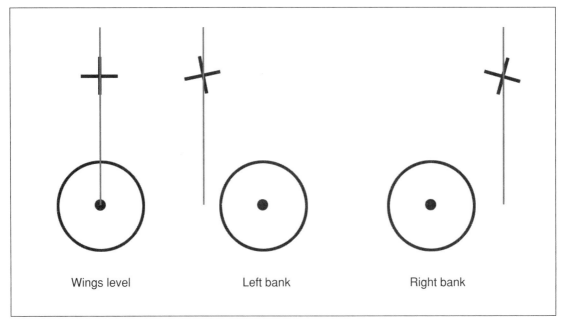

Wings level   Left bank   Right bank

Figure 4-10.
Pendulum effect

angle corrections will probably be needed, but get them done early in the pass to kill your 3/9 error. If you get close to the target and find you need to make large bank corrections, go through dry ("dry" is the term for making a weapons pass without releasing a weapon).

It is very hard to detect ground rush at the low approach angle normally associated with strafe and rocket attacks. At dive angles above 10 degrees it is easy to "feel" ground rush and pull away from the ground. At dive angles less than 10 degrees, however, by the time you feel the ground rush you're at eye level with the gophers. For this reason, you must pull the jet up and away from the target well before you detect the ground rising up to flatten you. Figure 4-11 shows a minimum-range strafe pass on a parked aircraft. Getting much closer than this could be fatal to your simulated self. JetFighter will give you a ground-clobber warning, but if you get this warning tone you're within a heartbeat of turning your jet into scrap metal.

Make sure you've killed your 3/9 errors early in the pass. Azimuth problems are the biggest reason why pilots miss when firing rockets or strafing. Banking the jet at endgame causes big problems. I have sat in the range tower and watched a number of fighter pilots make some strafe passes that look similar to a steering demo for a car commercial. All that was missing was the cones. In the real jet, these azimuth problems are usually caused by gusty crosswinds. In

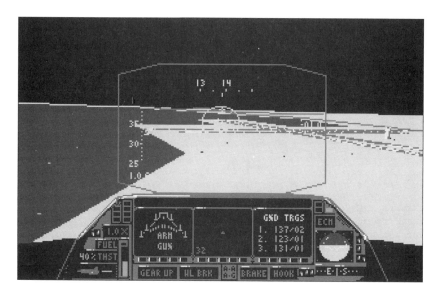

Figure 4-11. Strafe pass

JetFighter, these problems are caused by the pendulum effect. Remember, to avoid this problem, place the flight path marker under the target at roll-in.

After this lengthy discussion of strafe and rocket attacks, I have to admit that these deliveries are not very effective in JetFighter II. The major reason for this is that making a successful 20-mm strafe or KEM rocket attack is very difficult. KEM and 20-mm are hit-to-kill weapons. If you drop a bomb, there is a lethal blast and fragmentation radius of several hundred feet. With 20-mm and KEM, either you hit the target or you don't. You get no points for a near miss. The high degree of difficulty of the pass itself, coupled with the limited number of ground targets vulnerable to the 20-mm or the KEM, makes strafing and rocket attacks of limited use in JetFighter II. The good news on strafe and rocket deliveries in JetFighter II is that these attacks, even more than bombs, mirror the difficulty level of the same types of attacks in a real fighter. For this reason alone I like to strafe and shoot rockets in JetFighter II. In the real jet we call it "pipper discipline." This term refers to the mental discipline required to hold the pipper (the aiming dot in the reticle) on the target in order to get a hit. It's the same whether you're burning jet fuel or wall-socket electricity.

5 Countermeasures

Don't panic. Panic is your most formidable enemy.
—Major "Boots" Blessing, The Korean War Tactics Manual: No Guts—No Glory

Any discussion of JetFighter II countermeasures should start with the F-23 aircraft itself. The F-23, or Advanced Tactical Fighter, is an LO (low observable) aircraft which overcomes the poor maneuverability inherent in the boxy designs of first-generation LO aircraft. New next-generation engine technology gives the Advanced Tactical Fighter a supersonic cruise capability at thrust settings below AB, while an innovative airframe design, combined with vectored thrust, gives the F-23 unmatched maneuverability. The F-23 also features the latest in fighter avionics, including breakthrough data-link and radar technology. Among these impressive attributes, the Advanced Tactical Fighter's most important feature is LO. LO gives the F-23 pilot a tremendous air combat advantage. Complementing the LO features of the F-23 is a countermeasures suite that consists of chaff, flares, and a radar jammer. In this section we'll discuss the JetFighter II threat environment and how to use the features of the F-23 (and those of the other, less capable, fighters in the simulation) to survive and accomplish your missions in JetFighter II.

THE THREAT

The enemy in JetFighter II uses a modified form of Soviet Integrated Air Defense System (IADS), which consists of fighters, surface-to-air missiles (SAMs), and anti-aircraft artillery (AAA). Missiles are the primary threat to your longevity in JetFighter II. The enemy fires these missiles from the ground and from fighters. AAA is the next biggest threat to your jet in the simulation. AAA consists of ground-based large-caliber guns firing unguided explosive shells. The SAMs and AAA in JetFighter II are usually located at fixed sites in enemy territory, while the enemy fighters set up combat air patrols, or CAPs, at various locations over friendly and enemy territory. The enemy threat environment in the JetFighter II simulation (and in the real world) has three primary attributes. These are:

- Overlapping coverage
- Redundancy
- Connectivity

Overlapping coverage means that the enemy uses several weapons systems, with complementary capabilities, located on airborne platforms and at various ground sites. These platforms and sites are used to engage attacking aircraft with multiple systems simultaneously. *Redundancy* refers to the distributed nature of the threat. Even if you destroy some of the enemy's capabilities, you'll not completely destroy the entire enemy defense system. *Connectivity* means that if you're detected and engaged by one system, others may be alerted. This does not mean that the threat system is omniscient. What it does mean is that threat systems in JetFighter II show characteristics of real integrated air defense systems by passing information between different enemy platforms and sites. Detection by one type of enemy threat may raise your chances of being detected by other threat systems.

The first step the enemy IADS must accomplish before engaging your aircraft is detection. Once detection occurs, it engages the attacker with AAA or with a missile fired from a SAM site or a fighter. Detection in the JetFighter II simulation occurs the same way as it does on the modern battlefield—with radar systems. Ground- and air-based radar systems search the sky for the target. Once the target is detected, different radar systems, either airborne or ground-based, are used to track and engage the target. The entire enemy IADS, in the real world and in JetFighter II, leans heavily on radar for detection of targets. The massive U.S. Stealth technology effort was designed to cripple enemy radar base defenses. The F-23 is the latest in a successful line of combat aircraft that are very difficult (but not impossible) for enemy radar to detect over the battlefield. You may wonder why we would spend so much money on Stealth technology if an LO aircraft can still eventually be seen on radar. The reason is simple. Flying and fighting is the same as most other competitive endeavors in life: success is achieved on the margin. What this means is that there is a very slim line between success and failure. Small advantages usually produce big payoffs, and current U.S. LO technology is no small advantage. LO technology is, in fact, an enormous advantage that has made U.S. air power the dominant military force on the planet.

Even with the advantage produced by LO technology, your aircraft will sometimes be detected and engaged by threat systems. The next section describes these systems.

Surface-to-Air Missiles (SAMs)

JetFighter has two basic types of SAMs: radar-guided SAMs and infrared-guided (IR) SAMs. All of the radar-guided SAMs use an acquisition radar system to find your jet, then a tracking radar system to provide precise guidance information to the missile. You can think of radar as being very similar to a beam of light. A tracking radar illuminates your aircraft, allowing the guiding missile to see your aircraft and guide on it. The IR SAMs in JetFighter can also use acquisition and tracking radar to fire at your jet, but once the IR SAM is off the rail (fired), it self-guides to the target, using the IR energy generated by your engine.

Enemy Fighters

Enemy fighters are the most lethal threat that you face in JetFighter II (or in the real world). Enemy fighters use onboard intercept radar to find you, then they attempt to close in and shoot you down with IR- or radar-guided missiles. (Sound familiar?) The real difference between dealing with enemy fighters and enemy SAMs is that enemy fighters can mass their forces once they find you, while SAMs are stuck in fixed locations. This is the reason that fighters are more dangerous and difficult to deal with than SAMs. Ever since man has engaged in warfare, mobility and firepower have been the most critical combat attributes. Current fighter aircraft embody mobility and firepower in a way that no other combat system can match. You can think of an enemy fighter in JetFighter II as a highly mobile SAM site, which can latch onto your 6 o'clock and keep shooting missiles at you until you're dead.

The missiles fired by enemy fighters have essentially the same characteristics as the ones fired from the ground. In Chapter 3 we discussed what to do when an enemy aircraft fires a missile at your jet. The primary thing to remember here is that if you're detected by enemy fighters, you can expect more of them to be drawn to your location. You should take it very personally when an enemy fighter pilot, flying a Soviet built SU-27 like the one shown in Figure 5-1,

Figure 5-1. Su-27 fighter

closes in on your jet with evil intentions. When this occurs, you must focus your attention on killing him quickly and with style (see Chapter 3 for the stirring details of how to accomplish this task).

SAM sites, like the one shown in Figure 5-2, are manned by a bunch of ground-pounders, who we nickname "pounders," "shoe clerks," "grunts," and "poindexters." The kind of people who man SAM sites spend most of the time, when they are not gawking at a radar scope, playing with some unknown substance that came from a body orifice. Enemy fighters, on the other hand, are manned by fighter pilots like yourself. Air-to-air combat is the daring art of fighter pilot versus fighter pilot, with all the world's rewards at stake. The winner gets the spoils; the loser dies a noble death in mortal combat. The pounders at the SAM sites are dangerous, but they are still pounders and can be beaten more easily than fighter pilots (even in a simulation).

THE F-23

The F-23 is well equipped to survive the enemy IADS. This aircraft, featuring the latest LO technology, is very hard to find and shoot. There are a few things, however, that affect the observability of the F-23 in the JetFighter II simulation.

Figure 5-2. SA-6
Surface-to-Air Missile

- **Altitude.** The lower you fly, the harder it is for a radar system to pick you out of the clutter caused by the radar beam's hitting the ground.

- **Throttle position.** If you're in AB, you'll highlight yourself to the enemy's defenses.

- **Landing gear and the weapon bay doors.** Anything hanging out in the wind acts as a radar reflector and gives away your position to the enemy.

- **Jamming pod.** When you turn on the pod, your LO profile is blown.

F-23 Self-Defense Cockpit Displays

The F-23 cockpit has several key self-defense and countermeasure displays. These displays are shown in Figure 5-3. There are two Telelight panels, located on the far left and far right side of the cockpit. These lights are labeled in Figure 5-3. It is important to note that these lights are not labeled in the cockpit. You have to memorize the function of each of these lights so that in the heat of battle you can execute the correct response to the correct light. Fortunately this is not as hard as it sounds, because the Communications message panel, also labeled in Figure 5-3, will normally print out what is happening in clear text. In addition, JetFighter II gives you audio cues for an enemy missile launch.

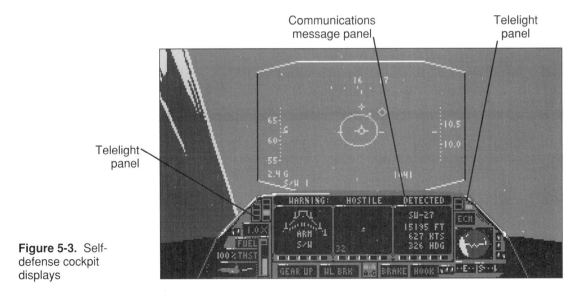

Communications
message panel

Telelight
panel

Telelight
panel

Figure 5-3. Self-
defense cockpit
displays

Left and Right Telelight Panels

The following list describes the lights on the Telelight panels and the
information each supplies. All of these lights are also accompanied by
a clear text message on the Communications message panel.

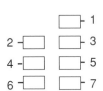

1. **SAM Launch Warning.** This light illuminates when a surface-
   to-air missile is off the ground and guiding on your jet.

2. **Infrared Missile Warning.** This light illuminates to tell you that
   an IR missile (fired from the ground or from an aircraft) is
   guiding on your aircraft.

3. **Radar Missile Warning.** This light illuminates to tell you that a
   radar missile (fired from the ground or from an aircraft) is
   guiding on your aircraft.

4. **Friendly Aircraft Detected.** This light illuminates when you lock
   the radar onto an aircraft that is identified as a "friendly." When
   you initially press [T] to lock the radar onto a target, the right
   MFD will initially display the target as unidentified. Figure 5-4
   shows the display that first appears when you lock onto a target.
   Once the radar IDs (identifies) the target, either the Friendly
   Aircraft Detected light or the Enemy Aircraft Detected light will
   illuminate.

5. **Enemy Aircraft Detected.** This light illuminates when the radar IDs the target you are locked onto as an enemy aircraft.

6. **Engine Fire Warning.** This light illuminates to indicate that you have a fire caused by battle damage. Fires are serious and normally require an ejection. If you wait too long to eject, you may lose that option and get torched.

7. **Hydraulic Failure Warning.** This light illuminates to indicate that battle damage has caused you to lose your hydraulic pressure. With this one, you can stay with the jet for as long as you can still control it. If you lose control, jump out.

There are additional lights on the right Telelight panel.

8. **Stall Warning.** This light tells the pilot that he has exceeded the stall Angle of Attack (AOA).

9. **Low Fuel Warning.** This light illuminates to let you know that you're about to become a glider pilot.

10. **Radar Observability Warning.** This light is on when you are no longer flying in Stealth mode. We've already discussed the pilot actions that will illuminate this light.

8 ⊣ ☐

9 ⊣ ☐   ☐ ⊢ 10

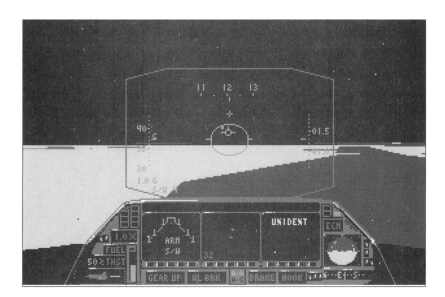

Figure 5-4. Enemy identification display

The Expendables: Chaff and Flares

The F-23 has a full complement of countermeasures to use against the enemy. The key to successfully employing these countermeasures is first to know their characteristics against the threat and, second, to have a way of using them that will work under pressure (remember the KISS principle—"Keep it simple, stupid!"). There are two general types of countermeasures used in modern fighters. These are expendables and onboard jammers. Expendables, as the name implies, are dropped from the aircraft, while jammers are carried on the jet and try to foil enemy radar or IR systems by transmitting jamming energy.

Chaff consists of tiny strips of metal, which rapidly bloom on release from the aircraft. A small explosive charge helps this process along. For chaff to be effective, it must quickly blossom into a radar-reflective cloud, whose size approximates that of the aircraft that dispensed the chaff. This cloud creates a false target and masks your jet to an enemy radar system. In the JetFighter simulation, you dispense chaff by hitting Ⓒ. When dispensing chaff, you'll get an audio indication that you have released chaff, along with a clear text message on the Communication message panel. The right MFD also has a Countermeasures Stores display that shows the pilot the number of chaff bundles and flares that remain in the aircraft. Figure 5-5 shows the Countermeasures Stores display. You can reach this

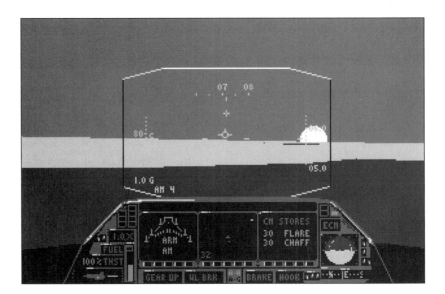

Figure 5-5. Chaff and flare counter

display quickly by pressing ⌈F6⌉. You can also step through the right MFD displays with ⌈F2⌉ until you get to this display. The F-23 carries 30 chaff bundles.

Flares are the other expendable carried by the F-23. Flares are simply pyrotechnic devices that give off heat in a specific micro-range to fool IR systems. In JetFighter, you dispense flares by pressing ⌈F⌉. Just as with chaff, you'll get an audio indication when you drop a flare, along with a clear text message on the Communications message panel. The F-23 carries 30 flares.

The Onboard Jammer

ECM, also called the radar jammer, is turned on by pressing ⌈J⌉. When activated, the ECM pod puts out jamming that acts primarily against an enemy tracking radar system. When the jammer is on, the ECM light (shown in Figure 5-6) illuminates, along with the Radar Observability warning light. Chaff and flares are considered passive jamming techniques, while all jamming that is transmitted from a pod is called active jamming. The difference is that when you start jamming with a pod, you're highlighting your jet. The F-23 jamming pod operates in what is known as a repeater mode. This means that it only transmits jamming energy when it detects radar signals with specific wave characteristics and intensity. When you actively jam

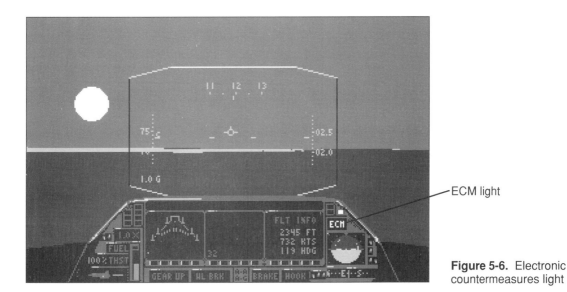

Figure 5-6. Electronic countermeasures light

with an LO fighter, however, you create a beacon in the sky for anybody with a radar system. That's the bad news. The good news is that you make it very hard for the bad guys to guide missiles onto you. Seeing you with an acquisition radar is not the same as holding a target-tracking radar system precisely on your jet and guiding a missile.

BATTLEFIELD SURVIVAL

To consistently survive in the JetFighter simulation you must have a tactical game plan for employing your countermeasures against the Integrated Air Defense System. You may have already discovered that you do not do your best creative thinking when the sky is full of missiles and you're down to your last 10 feet of altitude and 100 knots of airspeed. Remember, the IADS consists of a network of air- and land-based radar systems that are designed to detect incoming aircraft. Once they detect your jet, they track you and engage you with a missile. I call this the life cycle of an enemy engagement. The JetFighter pilot must have a tactical game plan that includes simple rules of thumb for handling each part of this enemy engagement life cycle.

The Detection Phase

One of the goals in every fighter mission is to prevent enemy acquisition or detection of your jet. LO aircraft such as the F-23 are well equipped to accomplish this goal. We have already talked about the pilot-controllable actions that can preserve your LO profile, the three primary ones being throttle position, altitude, and external devices. In JetFighter you should approach enemy territory below 500 feet or above 20,000 feet in a full LO condition. Below 500 feet, you are very difficult to detect on radar due to ground clutter and your Stealth characteristics.

When flying above 20,000 feet, you're above most of the AAA and, because of your Stealth features, you're still very hard to detect. At altitudes between 500 and 20,000 feet you may be engaged by optically aimed AAA. AAA gunners can find you with TV optics regardless of your Stealth characteristics, and AAA guns are accurate up to about 15,000 feet. AAA comes in two forms: aimed fire and barrage. In JetFighter, you'll notice that the AAA bursts are usually in close proximity to your jet. This means that the bad guys are using aimed fire. To spoil their aim you should use small random jinks, which are nothing more than changes of the aircraft velocity vector in both azimuth and altitude. The higher the altitude, the less drastic your jink needs to be. Remember that AAA is an aimed shell that has to be fired well out in front of your jet to score a hit. If you change your vector with the bullet in flight, you'll trash their shot. If you fly along on the same vector for the bullet's entire time of flight, then you may end up with a cockpit full of hair, teeth, and eyeballs. A good rule of thumb for altitudes above 10,000 feet is to jink every 5 seconds. For lower altitudes, jink every 2 to 3 seconds when you're in the midst of AAA. In every case, going faster will reduce the Pk (probability of kill) of AAA.

Target Tracking and Engagement

In JetFighter II, both the target tracking and engagement phases occur simultaneously. When a missile engages your aircraft, you have to react by using maneuvers and countermeasures. We have already discussed the cockpit lights that will illuminate when you are being engaged by a missile attack. Once you get one of these lights, you should immediately start a 90-degree bank 5- to 7-*G* turn for at least 45 degrees of heading change while dropping chaff or flares. Figure 5-7 shows this maneuver. The Communications message panel and the left Telelight panel will quickly inform you which type of missile

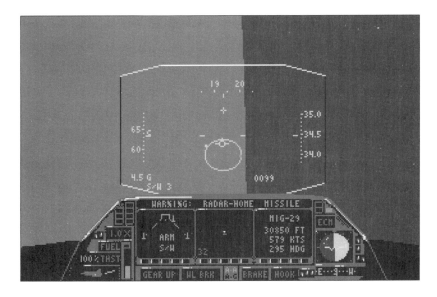

Figure 5-7. 90-degree high *G* turn

is heading your way, but if you're confused, drop one bundle of chaff and one flare and hold the new course for 5 to 10 seconds. After 5 to 10 seconds, roll up 90 degrees of bank, pull back to your original course, and resume the mission.

The center HSD display will show the missiles that have been fired at you. They appear as small squares, but they are sometimes hard to detect on the HSD if the scope is filled with other targets. Reducing to the 4-mile range scale will help you pick them out. Another option that you have against a radar missile is the jammer. If you maneuver the jet while feeding the missile a chaffburger and it still blows up next to your jet, then the next time a missile is fired you'll turn on your jammer by pressing ⓙ and then maneuver and drop chaff. The big problem with using the jammer is that you might forget to turn it off. Leaving a radar jammer on is like painting a "Shoot Me" sign on your aircraft.

Battle Damage

If you're hit by an enemy missile or AAA, you may or may not be seriously damaged. Serious damage will prevent you from performing your mission and may even cause you to give the jet back to the taxpayers (in other words, bail out). Not all AAA bursts and missile detonations close to your aircraft cause serious damage. So if you're under attack, you should keep executing your defensive measures until you're no longer under attack. At this point you can perform a battle damage check. A battle damage check is nothing more than checking your jet to see if you've been hit. You should first check your Telelight panel, and next check flight controls and engine response. Remember, the left Telelight panel has warning lights for a fire and a hydraulic failure. You can quickly check your flight controls by making a few gentle maneuvers. The engine response and thrust can be checked by moving the throttle back and forth and watching your RPM and airspeed.

If you have a problem, you need to go to the next step. Engine problems and flight stability problems can be overcome in some cases, but you should perform a controllability check before deciding to continue the mission. During this check, climb to 1000 feet or higher and make a few turns to check aircraft response. Last, *check your fuel.* One of the worst battle damage injuries you can sustain is a massive fuel leak. If your fuel cells have been turned to Swiss cheese, you'd better "get out of Dodge" before you end up flying a cinderblock.

The bottom line on battle damage is that you have to assess what you've lost and then make a call based on the tactical situation. Remember to keep fighting the incoming missiles first and check for battle damage when you are disengaged from the threat.

Threat Reaction

Reacting to the threat successfully requires the fighter pilot to have a few simple procedures that work when the pressure is on. We have discussed some simple steps that will help you exploit the countermeasure features of the F-23 in order to survive on the JetFighter battlefield. These steps are not the only ones that work, but they are based on real fighter threat reactions and they do meet the most important threat reaction requirement, in both real and simulated combat: they're easy to execute under pressure. I have seen many complex threat-reaction game plans fall apart in the air because they were too "cosmic." At zero airspeed they sounded good, but when you put the world on fast-forward by flying 1000 miles per hour, these cosmic plans just flat out don't work. The key to surviving the air battle is to think survival first and avoid detection if at all possible. Next, know your enemy, and when you are engaged, execute a straightforward threat-reaction plan that doesn't require too many brain-bytes to perform. In the mouth of the beast you won't have any to spare.

You may have noticed that we haven't discussed the other aircraft that you can fly in simulation. These aircraft are exactly the same as the F-23, with one big exception—they have no LO capability. When you're flying these aircraft, you'll have to go in low to avoid detection, and you'll definitely get engaged more often. All these aircraft still have chaff, flares, and radar jammers, and the same rules of thumb for threat reaction still apply.

In the next chapter, we'll go through a JetFighter mission and describe mission planning factors and pilot actions. This discussion will tie together our previous air-to-air, air-to-ground, and threat-reaction discussions, and will try to give you the "big picture" on JetFighter tactics.

6 Tactics

*He will win who knows
when to fight and when
not to fight.*
—*Sun Tzu,* The Art of War
(500 B.C.)

Getting off the runway turned out to be a standard "goat rope"—just as screwy as the whole week had been. The base at Cold Lake, Canada, has two parallel runways, so you'd think launching a strike package would be no problem. A Navy A-6 squadron, however, had aircraft problems all week long, causing them to taxi late and messing up the entire launch. Well, today turned out to be no different from the rest of the week, and I could tell by listening to those A-6 bozos whining on the radio that we were in for another "Curly and Moe" routine out in the arming area. I had plenty of gas on this mission, so I taxied out to the runway and took off early, avoiding most of the problems. Once I got my flight airborne I started to relax for the 10-minute cruise up to the start-route point northwest of the base.

My F-16 unit had deployed into the Royal Canadian Air Base at Cold Lake 5 days before to participate in a Maple Flag Exercise. Cold Lake is a beautiful chunk of earth located about 150 miles north of Edmonton, Alberta. The terrain consists primarily of rolling, pine-covered hills interrupted by hundreds of spectacular clear blue lakes. On the previous 3 days I'd flown air-to-air missions. This was my first "iron-hauling" mission, and I was leading a four-ship that was fragged (sent) to take out an industrial complex in the eastern part of the range complex. This "industrial complex" was really a few small wooden structures that stood in a clearing in the woods about as big as a football field.

My flight was part of a 40-aircraft package. Only four F-16s and four A-7s were going after the industrial complex. The rest of the bombers were four A-6s, eight F-16s, and eight F-111s and they were going after a variety of other targets in close proximity to our target area. The remaining 12 fighters were flying air-to-air and SAM suppression missions to support the strike. We got to the first point of the route early and entered a wide circular holding pattern to wait for the other aircraft in the strike package. Every flight had a "push time" when they were supposed to meet. What this means is that

each flight in the package was supposed to start the low level at a precise time. By meeting at this time, each flight would end up in its proper position in the formation.

My flight of four F-16s was on the pointy end of the sword as the strike package pushed off. Behind our four-ship stretched a 20-mile-long "gorilla" (a gorilla is a very large group of fighters that are flying within visual range of each other). Our four-ship was at the very front of this formation. The only aircraft that were in front of us were four F-15 Eagles that were flying an air-to-air sweep. We pushed exactly on time, and had just crested our first ridge line at 100 feet when the action started. AWACS had been calling bandits close to the package before we even got formed up, but I didn't worry too much about them because the flight of F-15s out in front of us had stripped from the package to engage.

As we got over the ridge, I got a radar contact on two high-aspect targets at high speed. Canadian F-18s were serving as enemy aircraft for this mission, so I figured it was the bad guys running an intercept on our formation. We had barely started the mission and these guys were already in our chili. What had happened to the Eagle sweep? Because the F-18 is a very formidable opponent, I broke away from the gorilla and started to run an intercept on the attacking bandits. Once an F-18 finds you on radar, you either run an intercept on him or wait for him to show up at your 6 o'clock. I chose not to wait. I sorted (detected) two targets in line-abreast formation at 15 miles on my radar, and immediately offset the flight up-sun (toward the sun) for a stern conversion. The aspect decreased, rapidly telling me that the bandits were not reacting to us, so at 8 miles I turned hot to bring the targets into the HUD. As we closed to 2 miles, I plainly saw the shape of the Hornet and fired a simulated Aim-9L. Just as I fired, both F-18s broke right into my formation at 8 *G*s and I passed beak-to-beak with the left-hand jet. I rolled up right 90 degrees and cranked my head around to check 6 (6 o'clock) and watch what they were doing, hoping this would not turn into a furball. They were thinking the same thing, and I picked up a tally (spotted the enemy) on four burner cans as they accelerated away.

Evidently they'd gotten a radar contact on the gorilla but had not sorted the entire formation. We ran in undetected until their threat warning alerted them that they were under attack. Getting ambushed by the guys that you're trying to ambush is no way to start to fight, so these guys just broke into us and then bugged out.

After that little soirée with the Hornets, I knew there would be no way to catch the gorilla and get back out in front of it. Luckily we had briefed an alternate TOT (time over target) for this type of situation. If you got engaged and stripped from the strike package, you just cycled into the target area after the gorilla had dropped its bombs. I typed this new TOT into the computer and got an airspeed carrot (a reference point on the airspeed scale on the HUD) that told me exactly how fast to fly to get to the target at this new time. The alternate TOT was 3 minutes after the main gorilla hit the target, so we changed our route to reach this target at the new later time. The brief fight with the F-18s had pushed us up to a higher altitude, so I descended back down into the weeds with my four-ship and continued on toward the mission.

Everything was going smoothly as we approached our target area. The air was calm and the radios were silent, with the exception of an occasional comment from AWACS on how there was nobody around. I felt good as our four-ship sliced peacefully through the sky toward our target. The birds in the trees below us were singing, God was in heaven, and all was right with the world. At the IP, I switched my system over to air-to-ground and we pressed in to attack the target. At 4 miles our flight started our pop-up attack with precision and confidence. Nothing could stop us. As I started to pull down toward the target, I glanced over at my wingman and my heart stopped. From my jet it appeared that he was flying right through a formation of A-7s. I keyed the mike to call him to turn to avoid them, but the call stuck in my throat as he flew right through their formation. Since there was no fireball, I glanced back toward the target and started my pull down for my attack. As I rolled out and dove for the ground, my HUD filled with two massive F-111s in a line-abreast formation. I rolled to the left and pulled, passing one of them too close for comfort. Again, my flight had literally dodged a bullet. At this point I was starting to get an uneasy feeling—what was going on here? Where were all these guys coming from? But pondering is not a fighter pilot specialty, so I continued my attack. At the instant when I was about to pickle, my wingman yelled, "Cobra 11 break right, F-18 at your 6 o'clock, closing."

Great, that was all we needed to make this air show over the target complete—F-18s diving into the fray. I started to break and tell my wingman that I had a tally-ho on the attacking F-18 when my UHF radio erupted into a deafening high-pitched squeal. Two of the

very lowest forms of life on this earth are serial killers and comm jammers. The worse of these two had found our frequency and was jamming our radios. My headset was filled with that deafening squeal as I futilely tried to answer my wingman and make sense of this world gone mad. The sky was filled with fighters going in every direction. The A-7s and F-111s we had already passed were part of the main gorilla, which had somehow arrived in the target area 3 minutes late. The sky is big, but it looked small as dozens of high-speed jets filled a 5-mile circle over the target area trying to find their targets. I drove straight ahead, afraid to move the jet for fear of hitting someone. In this type of situation, it's best to stay predictable . Aircraft passed through my HUD and flashed in and around me, and I lost track of my wingmen in the confusion. Just then, as if it had been meticulously planned, a threat radar found my jet and locked on. I picked up a faint missile launch warning through the comm jamming—good, a few simulated SAM launches to round out the scenario.

The radio squealed, the threat warning chirped out a muted warning, and my helmet visor reflected the tail numbers of almost every type of free-world fighter in the inventory. I fought to clear my head and focus on why I had arrived in this position in space and time. Oh yes, I'd come here to bomb a target. I was in the middle of a bad situation that I could do nothing to control, and since I was here anyway, I might as well bomb something. It couldn't get any worse. Just then I noticed that the steering in my HUD was pointing to a clearing in the trees off to my right that looked exactly like the target. I turned my attention away from the madness, took a deep breath, and rolled in.

The world stood still as I pickled and pulled away from the ground. I looked out on the wings to see if my bombs had come off clean, and noticed that I had one hung. It *could* get worse! Now I had a hung 500-pounder on the jet. The normal thing to do in this situation is to circle back into the target area and try an alternate bomb release. Well, as the saying goes, I may be crazy but I'm not stupid. No way was I going back into that chaos. I still couldn't talk on the radio, so I made myself as small as possible (think small and you'll be small) and put the steering to my egress point on my nose. My only goal at this point was to get my pink behind away from that "food fight," and do it in a hurry. Surprisingly enough, one of the jets in my flight arrived at the egress point at the same time as I did, with two A-7s that had lost the rest of the jets in their flight. We all formed into a four-ship box and headed for home. On the way out I found a nice lake and killed a few fish with the 500-pound bomb. The flight home was peaceful. We landed at Cold Lake "thinking about women and glasses of beer." Fighter pilots, luckily, are equipped with very short memories (along with other things). Either you're in one piece or you're not. If you make it through, then there's no need to dwell on it because if you think about it too long you'll only scare yourself and ruin a good night at the bar.

In the debrief I did find out that the gorilla had gotten engaged on the way to the target and had splintered into several separate flights. Some these flights had gotten engaged again, which delayed them even more. At least half of the jets in the strike package were trying to make the alternate briefed TOT that was 3 minutes after the primary TOT, and that was what caused the air show over the target.

I wish I could say that this mission was the most confused I have ever been in, in a fighter cockpit, but it was not. I also wish I could say that this was the most dangerous training mission I have ever been on but, again, it was not. This mission was not typical, but it was not unique either. Flying and fighting, even in training, is a dangerous and confusing endeavor. The thing to remember is that it will never go any better than the plan, but it may go far worse. With that in mind, you must make the best tactical plan possible and be ready to audible (to switch to a backup plan when your first plan starts to go bad). In this chapter we will discuss basic JetFighter mission planning factors, along with some rules of thumb for executing a mission plan. Just keep in mind that frequently your plan will not survive contact with the enemy.

MISSION PLANNING

The objective of most fighter missions is to destroy the enemy and survive. Figure 6-1 shows a scale depicting the balanced relationship between survival and target destruction. Simply put, a fighter pilot normally has to increase his exposure to the threat in order to accomplish the mission. The key to effective combat planning and execution is knowing when to favor one side of the scale at the

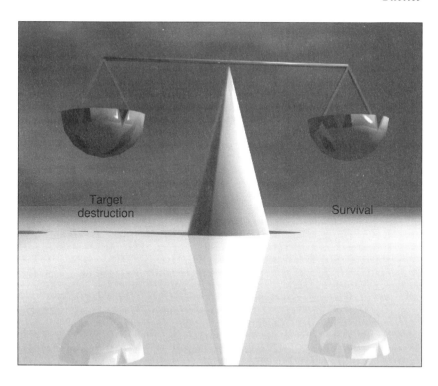

Figure 6-1. Target destruction versus survival

expense of the other. If you favor survival in the extreme, you'll never get near the enemy. If you favor target destruction too heavily, you may fail to react to an attacking enemy so you can complete your bombing run. A fighter pilot will normally keep the scale balanced during a mission. For brief periods of time, however, the scale will tip one way or the other.

Every JetFighter II mission presents the pilot with a challenging tactical situation. The pilot enters a combat mission by selecting the Adventure, Combat Missions, or Free Flight. Free Flight is a basic training mode, which allows control over some mission variables such as time of day, takeoff and landing runways, and the number of bandits airborne. To enter a tactical mission, the pilot must select the Adventure or the Combat Missions option. The Combat Missions mode allows access to over 100 independent missions, which are listed in the next chapter. Each mission has a specific threat environment and objective, but is not tied to any other mission. The Adventure uses the same missions, but they're all tied together in a tactical scenario. In other words, the results of one mission affect the outcome of the war. Statistics are kept and overall war strategy can be developed by the JetFighter II pilot. The next chapter lists the weight (or importance) of each of these missions in the war effort. An important part of the JetFighter II experience is entering the Adventure and developing your own strategy as you go. This chapter will not address overall war strategy because it's easy to use mission weights to select the most important missions. The difficult part of JetFighter II is actually planning and executing a mission once it has been selected.

The Mission Objective

Figure 6-2 shows a list of missions with one mission selected. This is where your mission planning starts. JetFighter II missions are delivered in very plain language. This plain language provides the target type, a report on enemy activity, and some useful suggestions on how to prosecute the mission. After reading your mission description, you can move on to the Weapons page. Before you do, however, you should digest your mission objective. JetFighter missions come in two basic flavors: air-to-ground and air-to-air. The air-to-ground missions are simple in concept: fly to a target and bomb it. You don't have to engage enemy aircraft to complete the mission; however, read your mission description carefully. When planning an air-to-ground mission you should minimize your

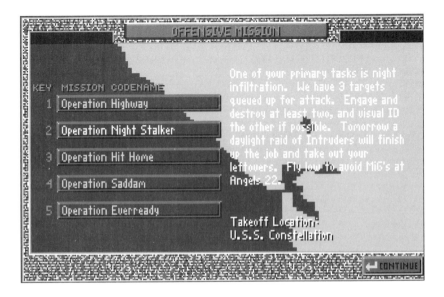

Figure 6-2. Mission list

exposure to threats. What this means is go fast and avoid confrontation with the enemy whenever possible. If the mission description suggests I get rid of the enemy aircraft in the area before bombing the target, however, then I will. If it says to avoid them or is silent on the matter, I'll leave them alone. Air-to-air missions come in two basic varieties: offensive counter air (OCA) and defensive counter air (DCA). DCA missions are the most challenging, and involve protecting something or someone from air attack. When you have a DCA mission, you should be prepared for a very fast-paced and challenging mission, in which mistakes in planning or execution will be very costly. OCA also involves killing enemy aircraft, but on these missions you're carrying the fight to the enemy and can dictate the timing and tempo of the mission. The enemy dictates the timing and tempo of a DCA mission. This has a very big impact on your planning and execution of the mission. When you are protecting something or someone, you'd better strap into that jet with a game plan in mind. On a DCA mission, the enemy may not allow you to ad lib.

Weapons

Figure 6-3 shows the Weapons page. On this screen you can select an aircraft type and the aircraft weapons load. For most air-to-ground JetFighter II missions, I select the Multi-role weapons configuration.

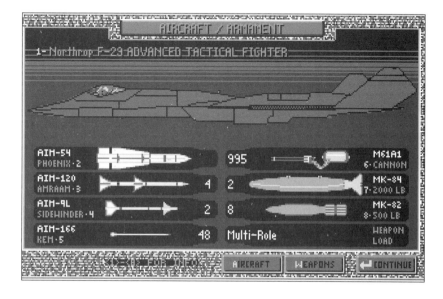

Figure 6-3. Weapons page

This will give you an adequate number of bombs and missiles to meet any combat contingency. If you're not good at manual bombing yet, then select the Ground Attack configuration, which will give you more bombs and fewer air-to-air missiles. If you have an air-to-air mission to fly, it's dealer's choice among the Fleet Defense, Long Range Dogfight, and Short Range Dogfight options.

Formulating the Mission Plan

Once you leave the Weapons page, you enter a Map view, which includes a repeat of the mission description text. Figure 6-4 shows this screen. This is where I form my plan for executing the mission. JetFighter II does not require more than a few minutes of planning, but if you spend these few minutes planning the mission, it will pay off once the shooting starts. Most of this screen is a map of the mission area. This screen does not show the target area or the SAM and AAA sites, but it does gives you the positions of the enemy aircraft. Using this Map view, you can plan your initial heading off the runway or the carrier. This heading will help you avoid enemy aircraft or will set you up for an intercept (depending on the tactical situation).

It is critical that you use this Map view to plan your intercept when flying a DCA mission. The map will not tell you the altitude or the bandit type, but it will give you the enemy attack formation.

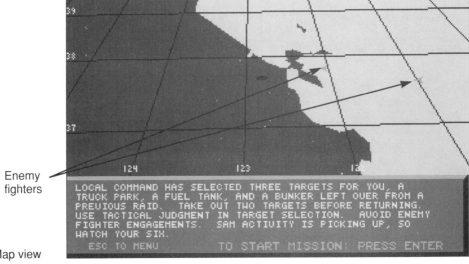

Enemy
fighters

Figure 6-4. Map view

With this information, you should plan an initial "min time to ram" attack heading on the bandits so that you don't wallow around and waste time once you get airborne.

Cockpit Setup

When you press Enter in this Map display, the mission begins. Upon entering the cockpit, you immediately set up the cockpit in the configuration that you need for the mission. Figure 6-5 shows the initial cockpit displays for an air-to-ground mission. I rarely take off with the GND TRGS display in the right MFD. When enemy aircraft are present on the Map view before you enter the cockpit, you fly with the AIR TRGS display in the right MFD. If the enemy aircraft are outside of 15 miles, leave the HSD on the 32-mile range scale. If they're inside of 15 miles, change the scale to 15 miles. If bandits are within 15 miles when you enter the cockpit, you should also call up your AMRAAMs by pressing Enter . If the bandits are outside of this range, don't call up a weapons mode until you get airborne and set up your intercept. Calling up a weapon opens the bay doors and blows your LO profile. Setting up the cockpit before you take off is good idea, but you should note that the mission starts when you enter the cockpit. If you just sit there on the ground dithering, an enemy aircraft or Cruise missile will sneak up on you and rearrange your dental work.

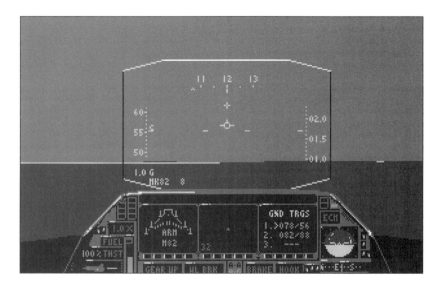

Figure 6-5. Air-to-ground cockpit displays

MISSION EXECUTION

The planning stage is over when you run up the engine for takeoff. From this point on you need to think execution (of both the plan and the enemy). Execute your tactical game plan and change it when (not if) the tactical situation changes. In this section we will cover the various JetFighter II mission types, along with some techniques for executing the missions.

Defensive Counter Air (DCA)

DCA missions can be the most difficult missions to execute in JetFighter II because the enemy dictates the timing and tempo of the mission. There are a few things that the pilot can do to succeed in a fast-paced DCA scenario. In the planning stage, we discussed getting your cockpit switches set up and getting ready to turn directly toward the enemy. It is important in a DCA mission that you sort the enemy as fast as possible. A sort is an attempt to determine the following information on enemy aircraft:

- The formation in which they're flying
- The number of enemy aircraft in the formation
- The altitude of the enemy aircraft
- Enemy intentions

The JetFighter II mission planning stage will tell you the number of enemy aircraft and their formation. Figure 6-6 shows a Map view

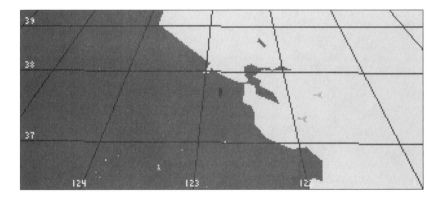

Figure 6-6. Map view of a formation of enemy targets

with a formation of enemy air targets. What you don't know is what type of enemy aircraft are inbound and at what altitude they're flying. Enemy intentions in JetFighter II are usually easy to discern. On a DCA mission, the enemy just comes straight at the target.

To successfully sort the enemy, you need to get within 32 miles and start locking onto the enemy aircraft, using the T key. Remember that the target you're locked onto will flash. Once you're locked onto the target, the AIR TRGS display will give you the target type, altitude, speed, and heading. On a DCA mission it is critical that you find the Cruise missiles, if there are any in the enemy formation, and set up to take them out first. To find them you need to "step" the radar through the entire enemy formation, using the T key. Make a mental picture of the enemy attack profile. Figure 6-7 shows an attacking enemy formation. If all of the Cruise missiles are at low altitude, you should climb to no higher than 5000 feet for your intercept. If they're running with an altitude split, as shown in Figure 6-7, then climb to co-altitude with the high target and take it out first. Use your altitude to descend on the low target after

Figure 6-7. Attacking enemy formation

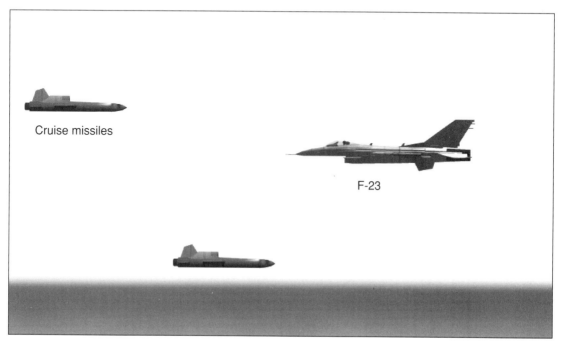

Cruise missiles

F-23

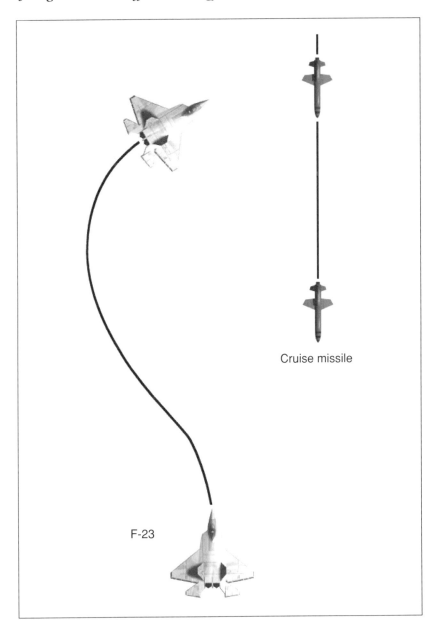

Figure 6-8. Correct attack geometry on an inbound Cruise missile

splashing the high target. Figure 6-8 shows a good attack geometry on an inbound Cruise missile.

As a rule of thumb, you want to close with the nearest target quickly, then slow down to control the engagement once you arrive within visual range.

Offensive Counter Air

On these air-to-air missions in JetFighter, you can actually control the timing and tempo of the engagement. In a DCA mission, you have to protect something, so you have very constrained engagement criteria. Get to the target as quickly as possible. OCA missions in JetFighter II can be equally important, but you have more control over how you perform them. Here are some rules of thumb:

- Run a stern conversion intercept on the targets.
- Keep your LO profile until you're at the bandit's 6 o'clock.
- Perform a good sort and prioritize your targets.
- Once you've taken out the primary target, don't stay in a fight unless you have the advantage.
- Even if you haven't taken out the primary target, separate from the fight if you lose the advantage.

Ground Attack Missions

Ground attack missions encompass elements of air-to-air as well as air-to-ground combat. The key to successfully executing these missions is to know when to engage an enemy fighter and when to avoid him. During the mission planning stage, you should read the mission description for intelligence on dealing with enemy fighters. In addition, once you are airborne, you should not plan a route of flight that takes you around known threats. After taking off on a ground attack mission, you have two choices of ingress profiles: the low-altitude option, at 500 feet and below, and the medium-altitude option, which will take you in above 20,000 feet. Altitudes in between will put you in the AAA envelope. Before choosing between the low and high profiles, you should note the mission intelligence briefing concerning enemy aircraft. If the mission advises you to avoid contact with the enemy, then fly low. If you are advised to take out enemy fighters before bombing, go in high. Going in low is usually your best bet overall, because it is easy to both avoid detection and hit the target when flying at low altitude.

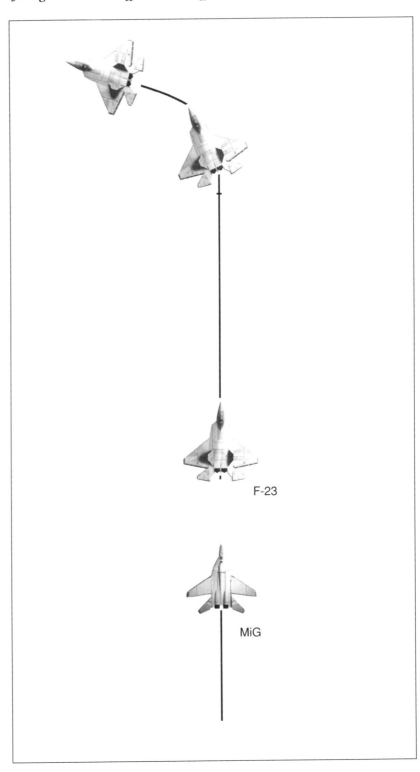

Figure 6-9. Run in AB then a change of course as you cancel AB

TACTICAL PERSPECTIVE

If you are detected by enemy fighters while flying an air-to-ground mission, then you have two choices: run or fight. If you're flying the F-23, you're flying the fastest jet in the air battle. The problem is that you have to use burners to outrun the enemy, and when you light the AB you're no longer stealthy. For this reason, when you're initially detected, you can run in full AB until you're about 5 to 7 miles from the bandit, then terminate AB and change your course. Figure 6-9 shows this profile. If the enemy still has a grip on you after this maneuver, then turn around and engage him.

All fighter pilots have their own unique techniques for dealing with tactical situations; these are called tactical perspectives. In this chapter we discussed some JetFighter planning factors and a few rules of thumb for mission execution. Your job now is to modify these techniques to fit your own tactical perspective. My techniques for flying and fighting in JetFighter II have been shaped by flying the F-4, the A-7, and the F-16. This experience gives me with some advantages, along with some limitations. Fighter pilots are nothing more than products of their training. For example, based on my training over the last 10 years, I like to go into the target area at low altitude. You may have noticed that in the Gulf War there was very little low-altitude flying. In fact, the F-117s came in at medium altitude. It is hard for me, however, to fly at medium altitude in JetFighter with people shooting at my jet. The urge to descend is overwhelming. The average JetFighter pilot can develop his own techniques, free of these naturally inbred "urges." You should follow your own instincts and use our discussions in this manual as a starting place to build your own unique JetFighter tactical perspective.

Good hunting!

7 Mission Summaries

*Only the dead have
seen the end of war.*
—*Plato*

Now that you've studied the JetFighter II weapons and tactics, you have all the knowledge you need to fight and win the JetFighter II Adventure. This chapter will provide the details for each mission, including some specific mission tactics. For each mission, its Strategic Value is listed under its title. The Strategic Value assigned to each mission is a point value, awarded to you when you complete the mission objectives. Selecting missions with the highest Strategic Values will give you the highest payoff when fighting the Adventure air campaign. (It's very hard to guess which missions will have the greatest impact on the war, though, because the pilot isn't given enough strategic information to figure that out.)

Targeting is a very complex and time-consuming task, but here are some general rules of thumb that apply when picking targets in a real air war. The first missions flown are Defensive Counter Air (DCA), Offensive Counter Air (OCA), and Suppression of Enemy Air Defenses (SEAD). Command and Control nodes that are part of the enemy air defense system are struck first, along with acquisition radar sites. Next come individual surface-to-air missile (SAM) sites and airfields. Enemy aircraft are engaged in the air and bombed on the ground in the OCA campaign. While SEAD and OCA missions are under way, DCA missions are flown to protect friendly airspace. The goal of the air campaign is to gain and maintain air superiority. Once this is achieved, air power can be directed against enemy tactical and strategic targets (the terms *tactical* and *strategic* refer only to the targets, not to the aircraft engaging the targets). Tactical targets are those that are in and around the battlefield, and strategic targets are those that affect enemy war-making capability, such as factories and power plants.

In JetFighter II you're thrust into an air campaign that's already under way. You don't have critical information about the overall war effort, so it's hard to find out how your side is doing in the fight for air superiority. To make your mission selection simple, use the Strategic Value numbers to pick your missions.

MISSION 1: Missile Attack
STRATEGIC VALUE: 15
TAKEOFF TIME: 17:49
TAKEOFF LOCATION: U.S.S. Constellation
ORDERS: Scramble immediately to intercept two sea-skimming missiles launched toward the carrier. Splash both bandits so we don't have to rely on the Phalanx guns. These missiles travel low and fast, so watch your speed and don't give the taxpayer's aircraft a salt-water bath.

MISSION 2: Lost Lamb
STRATEGIC VALUE: 15
TAKEOFF TIME: 04:52
TAKEOFF LOCATION: U.S.S. Constellation
ORDERS: A lone bandit has strayed into our patrol area. Intercept and destroy this target. There's a chance that he's carrying an Exocet, so don't waste any time. Splash him before he gets close enough for a launch.

MISSION 3: Two for Tea
STRATEGIC VALUE: 15
TAKEOFF TIME: 06:37
TAKEOFF LOCATION: U.S.S. Constellation
ORDERS: AWACS just picked up two bandits returning from a previous engagement. They're probably low on fuel and armament. Intercept and destroy. But watch out—these guys just splashed some of our boys. Now it's payback time!
TACTICS: When you take off, the bogeys will be outside of 32 miles, so you'll need to use Map view information for your initial intercept vector. This vector should be approximately 090 degrees. Expect IR SAMs on this mission, and be ready for IR SAM countermeasures. Don't forget that approaching SAMs are visible as white dots on your HSD. At the 4-mile range setting, you can get instant feedback on the effects of your countermeasures. When you get within 32 miles of the bandits, do a sort. You'll notice that both of the targets are high (about 40,000 feet), so get your carcass up there with them so you don't start the fight with an energy disadvantage. The guys flying these jets are no radar wizards, so you should be able to execute a stealthy intercept and a brutal ambush.

MISSION 4: Easy Pickings
STRATEGIC VALUE: 15
TAKEOFF TIME: 05:36
TAKEOFF LOCATION: U.S.S. Constellation
ORDERS: Three bandits returning from aerial practice maneuvers are getting brave and wandering into the hot zone. These are rookie pilots without much training. Go ahead and show them who owns this airspace. Keep an eye out for their instructor, though.

MISSION 5: ATF Stolen!
STRATEGIC VALUE: 17
TAKEOFF TIME: 15:15
TAKEOFF LOCATION: U.S.S. Constellation
ORDERS: We have a sensitive situation. An F-23 has been stolen by either an impostor or a spy. The Black Widow is meeting up with a MiG escort. Needless to say, you *must* destroy the ATF before the enemy can take it apart. The F-23 was unarmed, so watch the MiGs and splash that aircraft!

MISSION 6: Sitting Ducks
STRATEGIC VALUE: 6
TAKEOFF TIME: 01:28
TAKEOFF LOCATION: U.S.S. Constellation
ORDERS: A regularly scheduled convoy of transports is passing through the area. Knock out all the aircraft and return to base. These ships carry ammo and repair parts for the SU-27, so don't take this mission lightly. Watch for heavy SAM cover.

MISSION 7: MiG Patrol
STRATEGIC VALUE: 6
TAKEOFF TIME: 01:28
TAKEOFF LOCATION: U.S.S. Constellation
ORDERS: Scramble immediately to intercept a patrol of two MiGs entering our sector. This may be an attempt to launch anti-ship missiles, or the MiG patrol may just be off course. Splash both bogeys, then return to the carrier.

MISSION 8: Operation Everready
STRATEGIC VALUE: 11
TAKEOFF TIME: 20:30
TAKEOFF LOCATION: U.S.S. Constellation
ORDERS: Our primary goal in the north sector is to cut supply lines. The enemy has munitions caches and truck depots scattered throughout the sector. Take out at least one of two targets and return safely to base. Watch for enemy fighter cover and SAM activity. Any remaining targets will be mopped up tomorrow.
TACTICS: Enemy aircraft in this mission are flown by the little old ladies who fly auxiliary, so if you want to raise your kill total, go ahead. SAMs won't be a problem as you whack those MiGs, because they're being operated by graduates from the Iraqi Air Defense School. Just finding the launch button is a challenge for these guys. This mission is an excellent time to hone your air-to-air skills. Also, if you're just beginning to learn how to manual-bomb, you may find it easier to go after the munitions caches. An enemy transport depot is much harder to see, even at 1000 feet. When in doubt about target location, bomb whatever is under the air-to-ground TD box.

MISSION 9: Operation Dig Out
STRATEGIC VALUE: 12
TAKEOFF TIME: 09:26
TAKEOFF LOCATION: U.S.S. Constellation
ORDERS: It looks like the enemy is getting overconfident and has started constructing command bunkers this far north. You have to take out two bunkers rumored to be nearing completion. Get target heading and distance from your Ground Targets display. Use a 1000-lb bomb to assure destruction. SAM and ground fire should be moderate.
TACTICS: The orders suggest the use of Mark-84 2000-lb bombs to destroy the target, but Mark-82s work just as well if you hit the target. Go after target #2 first, then bomb target #1. The threat in this mission has the I.Q. of a philodendron, so you can use countermeasures and just fly the mission. All you have to do to beat the threat on this mission is avoid getting hit by unguided SAMs.

MISSION 10: Operation Fourth of July
STRATEGIC VALUE: 22
TAKEOFF TIME: 18:00

TAKEOFF LOCATION: U.S.S. Constellation

ORDERS: Intelligence reports that weapons production has moved into several small makeshift factories in the sector. We expect to find a lot of unprotected explosives being warehoused. Score two of three targets. Let's make some pretty fireworks!

TACTICS: On this mission, bomb targets #2 and #3 first. They're closest to the carrier, and relatively close to each other. The MiG-29 in this mission has a good pilot—he'll fight aggressively when engaged. If you have to fight, try to kill him at the first pass.

MISSION 11: Operation Highway

STRATEGIC VALUE: 8

TAKEOFF TIME: 19:43

TAKEOFF LOCATION: U.S.S. Constellation

ORDERS: Hope you're ready for some multi-role duty! We need some munitions depots taken out. Be careful—enemy fighter cover has been particularly annoying lately. Destroy two of three targets and splash any intruding aircraft. Luckily, SAM activity is low this far north.

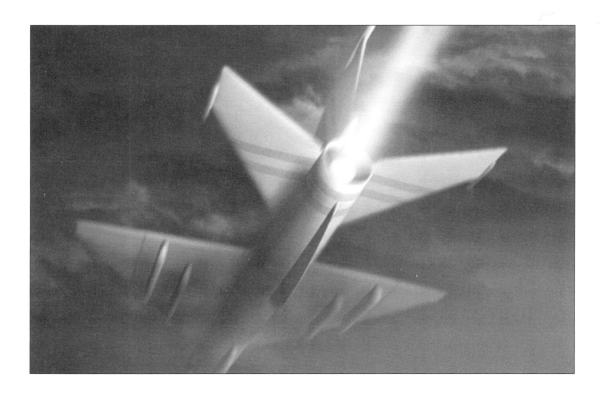

MISSION 12: Operation First Strike
STRATEGIC VALUE: 12
TAKEOFF TIME: 18:02
TAKEOFF LOCATION: U.S.S. Constellation
ORDERS: In order to prevent further movement northward, we've targeted several fuel tanks that the enemy uses for front-line refueling. Take out all three targets before returning. Fighter cover has been light, but watch your back.

MISSION 13: Operation Airlift
STRATEGIC VALUE: 20
TAKEOFF TIME: 21:57
TAKEOFF LOCATION: U.S.S. Constellation
ORDERS: The enemy is getting daring and is trying to resupply troops via transport landings at SFO. Approach SFO and destroy any heavy aircraft in the area. Watch for heavy activity from portable SAM and anti-aircraft installations. Good luck!
TACTICS: Take off and turn right to a heading of 130 degrees to proceed to the target area. During your approach to the San Francisco area, be prepared for an IR SAM engagement. Enemy air defense is light this far north, so IR SAMs are probably all you'll encounter. Don't forget your IR countermeasures when you're engaged by this threat. MiGs shouldn't be a problem during your approach, but stay heads-up for low-altitude AAA. The targets are aircraft in the open at San Francisco International—a fighter pilot's dream! You can only hope that they're fully fueled and armed when your bombs hit them. These targets are also vulnerable to a strafe or rocket attack, so let them have it.

MISSION 14: Operation Roach Motel
STRATEGIC VALUE: 14
TAKEOFF TIME: 07:23
TAKEOFF LOCATION: U.S.S. Constellation
ORDERS: The enemy is shipping fuel from local storage tanks via regular utility trucks. Each truck is packed with oil drums, so when you hit them, get out quick or the blast will rock your socks off. Destroy two of three targets before returning.
TACTICS: These targets are small and hard to hit, but as the saying goes, this is no hill for a climber. Enemy air activity is light, so you can take your time on this attack. Use the level bomb technique we

discussed in Chapter 4. Since the targets are so hard to ID, you may have to lean heavily on the avionics on this one. Still, the selected target on the right MFD will appear under the TD box. If all else fails during the level bomb attack, as the TD box starts to pass under the nose, pickle! With the TD box you don't even have to see a target to hit it.

MISSION 15: Operation Tin Can
STRATEGIC VALUE: 12
TAKEOFF TIME: 21:50
TAKEOFF LOCATION: U.S.S. Constellation
ORDERS: We've located two possible command bunkers, which need to be neutralized. Also, clean up a fuel tank that may be supplying their forces. Patrols of heavily armed bandits have been crisscrossing the area. Try to avoid them at all costs. Wax two of three targets. Tomorrow's F-18s will take care of the rest.

MISSION 16: Operation Sand Trap
STRATEGIC VALUE: 21
TAKEOFF TIME: 15:01
TAKEOFF LOCATION: U.S.S. Constellation
ORDERS: We've been pounding their bunkers hard, and they're alert to our tactics, but we still need to take out two more targets—a bunker and a local depot. You also have to splash *any* bandits in the area. Good luck and watch your 6.

MISSION 17: Birds of a Feather
STRATEGIC VALUE: 9
TAKEOFF TIME: 09:08
TAKEOFF LOCATION: U.S.S. Constellation
ORDERS: Intercept and destroy an aerial convoy before it has a chance to exit the sector. The last several of these convoys have been very lightly escorted due to our recent air-to-air victories in the north. However, watch for MiG cover. Anti-aircraft should be light so they don't clobber their own birds.
TACTICS: After takeoff, turn to an initial heading of 110 degrees for the intercept. The enemy aircraft are fleeing southeast, so check the Map view and make your correction to achieve a cut-off vector. During the intercept you'll be engaged by IR SAMs, so be ready to feed them a few flares. As you get within 32 miles, do a sort by

pressing T. By cycling through the targets, you can find out if there are any wolves hidden in among the sheep. In this case there is one, so you need to find him and kill him. Take him out with a BVR AMRAAM shot if possible. Once you've splashed the lone escort, you can have your way with the sheep. This is a great mission for practicing your KEM shoots against air targets. The IL-96 transports are slow, and fly straight and level. You should approach them from behind when making a KEM attack, and slow to match their speed.

MISSION 18: Operation Hit Home
STRATEGIC VALUE: 12
TAKEOFF TIME: 08:22
TAKEOFF LOCATION: U.S.S. Constellation
ORDERS: Until now, the enemy has ignored Oakland International as being too close to the eastern front. However, recent troop movements suggest they may be invading the area. Unfortunately, we have to render OAK useless to prevent their advance. Bomb the main runways into dust.

MISSION 19: Operation Tonka
STRATEGIC VALUE: 22
TAKEOFF TIME: 12:59
TAKEOFF LOCATION: U.S.S. Constellation
ORDERS: Satellite recon shows truck convoys moving south from what we suspect to be a missile parts depot. Because of our recent progress, the enemy is evacuating these high-tech components south. Take out at least one target. Further patrols will clear the rest. AAA has been heavy lately.

MISSION 20: Operation Night Stalker
STRATEGIC VALUE: 12
TAKEOFF TIME: 23:18
TAKEOFF LOCATION: U.S.S. Constellation
ORDERS: One of your primary tasks is night infiltration. We have three targets lined up for attack. Engage and destroy at least two, and visually ID the other if possible. Tomorrow a daylight raid of Intruders will finish up the job and take out your leftovers. Fly low to avoid MiGs at Angels 22.

MISSION 21: Operation Hunter
STRATEGIC VALUE: 17
TAKEOFF TIME: 22:47
TAKEOFF LOCATION: U.S.S. Constellation
ORDERS: You have to hunt down and destroy tonight's shipment of small-arms ammo. Locate and destroy two convoys of trucks evacuating these supplies south. Even a near-miss should touch off their loads if our intelligence is correct. Watch for high-flying fighter patrols and avoid them if possible.
TACTICS: This is a standard bombing mission. The twist on this one is that to successfully complete the mission you have to kill the bandit.

MISSION 22: Operation No Mercy
STRATEGIC VALUE: 14
TAKEOFF TIME: 04:40
TAKEOFF LOCATION: U.S.S. Constellation
ORDERS: The enemy is sending damaged fighters south for repairs. Intelligence reports that most, if not all, of these fighters are unarmed, and some have limited maneuverability. Join an F-18 in flight and destroy all the fighters before returning to base. Watch for a live one . . . good luck!
TACTICS: On this mission you get to fly in close proximity to another friendly aircraft. Close with the enemy at full AB. As you complete your intercept, shoot as fast as you can. The enemy aircraft on this mission are all grapes (with one exception). Watch your gas on this mission—a prolonged food fight could get you into trouble.

MISSION 23: Operation Saddam
STRATEGIC VALUE: 25
TAKEOFF TIME: 11:59
TAKEOFF LOCATION: U.S.S. Constellation
ORDERS: Our eyes in the sky have found shipping activity around two structures. Civilians confirm that two small electronics plants have been converted into munitions holding facilities. Completely destroy at least one of these. Leftovers will be cleaned up by tomorrow's A-6 patrols.

MISSION 24: Operation Last Call
STRATEGIC VALUE: 18
TAKEOFF TIME: 16:45
TAKEOFF LOCATION: U.S.S. Constellation
ORDERS: Intelligence reports confirm that a local adhesives factory is being converted to produce chemical weapons in a last-ditch effort to secure this sector. Take out the plant and at least one of two feeder facilities. Avoid enemy air cover.

MISSION 25: Operation Grand Slam
STRATEGIC VALUE: 20
TAKEOFF TIME: 23:16
TAKEOFF LOCATION: U.S.S. Constellation
ORDERS: A variety of targets have presented themselves. Take out suspected weapons plant, truck park, and fuel tank. Destroy all targets. You'll be flying low under cover of darkness. Try to dodge high-flying fighter patrols.

MISSION 26: Fleet Defense (easy)
STRATEGIC VALUE: 5
TAKEOFF TIME: 04:30
TAKEOFF LOCATION: U.S.S. Constellation
ORDERS: Multiple targets are reported inbound from several different locations. Current headings suggest that they're converging on the carrier. Possible attempt to launch a Exocet anti-ship missile. Intercept and destroy all inbound targets. Consult AWACS download for target locations and types.
TACTICS: The carrier exists primarily to defend itself. Over half the air power deployed on a carrier is used for self-preservation. After the CAT shot, the targets attacking your ship will be straight ahead. Inside the first minute of your intercept (flown at full AB), the first two targets will appear on your HSD. The closest target is an SU-27, but before you engage it, you have to make a decision. Remember from the orders that there may be an Exocet launch on your carrier, so do a sort of all targets on the HSD. After sorting the targets you'll see that the trailer (the farthest target in the two-ship formation) is an Exocet missile. You can and should engage the SU-27 in the lead, but don't turn with him. Give him an AMRAAM shot in the lips and blow by to engage the Exocet. You can pass the SU-27 at high aspect and then run a stern conversion on the Exocet. This will allow you to

take multiple shots from 6 o'clock and raise your Pk (probability of kill).

MISSION 27: Deaf, Dumb, and Blind
STRATEGIC VALUE: 14
TAKEOFF TIME: 23:04
TAKEOFF LOCATION: U.S.S. Constellation
ORDERS: Launch and immediately intercept three bogeys straying into our area. SAC recommends stealthy closure. These bogeys may be having radar/nav software difficulties, since they seem to be unaware of our presence.

MISSION 28: San Fran Incoming!
STRATEGIC VALUE: 14
TAKEOFF TIME: 12:53
TAKEOFF LOCATION: Oakland International
ORDERS: Engage immediately and destroy multiple cruise missiles inbound toward San Francisco. New AWACS systems have a good track on these missiles, so closure should be easy. Don't let them hit our beautiful city!
TACTICS: This is a tough one if you don't know the ropes in advance. The key to this mission is a good target sort. You have to get airborne and find the Cruise missiles. Once you're locked onto a Cruise missile, fly a stern conversion and shoot them down fast. This mission is very straightforward once you develop your radar sorting skills. At the start of the mission, several important tactical events will draw your attention. To your right, three Cruise missiles are skimming over the ground toward downtown San Francisco. These missiles are your targets. If you miss the intercept, they'll become part of the new city remodeling plan. A friendly B-757 is also flying around off to the west—it will distract you if you haven't sorted the primary targets. A MiG-29 Fulcrum is at your 6 o'clock. In order to succeed on this mission, you have to get in tune with the timing and tempo being created by the incoming Cruise missiles. To do this you have to focus your attention on finding them, performing an intercept, and then destroying them. Have your avionics configured before you roll for takeoff. The HSD should be in 15-mile or 4-mile scope and you should have your AMRAAMs selected. As you close with the Cruise missile, note its airspeed on the right MFD and match this speed once you get within firing range. If you don't

control your speed, you'll blow right by them. The MiG-29 at your 6 o'clock will probably engage you, but you'll have to trust your countermeasures and a few small, tight high-*G* turns. If you get wrapped up defensively with this guy you'll miss the intercept.

MISSION 29: Playground Boss
STRATEGIC VALUE: 14
TAKEOFF TIME: 03:12
TAKEOFF LOCATION: U.S.S. Constellation
ORDERS: AWACS and ground radar have located three bogeys loitering in our area. They may be another local patrol, or they may have their eyes on the carrier. Intercept and destroy any hostile targets you can. Support will be launched to clean up your leftovers.

MISSION 30: Missiles Inbound
STRATEGIC VALUE: 14
TAKEOFF TIME: 14:33
TAKEOFF LOCATION: San Francisco International
ORDERS: NORAD has detected two missile launches from the Livermore area. These may be ground-launched Cruise missiles. AWACS also show a bandit in the area, which could be missile cover. Intercept and destroy at all costs. This could be a move on the carrier.

MISSION 31: SFO Under Attack
STRATEGIC VALUE: 14
TAKEOFF TIME: 14:33
TAKEOFF LOCATION: Oakland International
ORDERS: *Emergency*! Scramble immediately to intercept three inbound Cruise missiles. The targets seem to be heading directly toward SFO! If these missiles are anti-runway devices, they could render San Francisco International useless!

MISSION 32: Hornet Harassed
STRATEGIC VALUE: 14
TAKEOFF TIME: 14:33
TAKEOFF LOCATION: Oakland International
ORDERS: Immediately intercept bandit engaging friendly F-18 near Livermore. Allied F-18 is known to be low on armament, so go full-AB to intercept. Watch for other MiG cover in the area. Destroy any enemy MiGs you encounter.

TACTICS: Escort missions are tough and this one is no exception. You have to intercept the attacking enemy aircraft as soon as possible, so take off in AB and turn to a 180-degree heading as soon as you're airborne. As you get airborne there will be some nuisance AAA just south of the airport, but don't let it distract you. Get the jet ready for an air-to-air fight, because time is of the essence. As the targets appear on your HSD, do a good sort to pick the correct bandit to engage first. The target to the left is the allied F/A-18. As you approach, you'll notice one of the bandits pursuing the F/A-18. Go after this bandit, because if he shoots down the F/A-18 that's the ballgame. While you're engaging this bandit, there's another one at your 6 o'clock. Take out the first one, then turn to engage the one at 6 o'clock.

MISSION 33: Operation Grenade
STRATEGIC VALUE: 15
TAKEOFF TIME: 19:00
TAKEOFF LOCATION: Oakland International
ORDERS: Target and destroy two truck-loading areas that move explosives from factories to the front-line ground forces. These parts go directly into new grenades, which have taken their toll on our ground troops. Destroy any enemy air cover present.
TACTICS: An enemy fighter will shadow you as you attack your ground targets during this mission. If he gets within 4 miles, it's best to turn and engage him.

MISSION 34: Operation Proud Deep
STRATEGIC VALUE: 10
TAKEOFF TIME: 13:43
TAKEOFF LOCATION: U.S.S. Constellation
ORDERS: A regularly scheduled maintenance flight of MiGs is starting near San Jose. Pursue and destroy enemy airborne targets. They should be low on armaments and off guard. After you finish them off, destroy one or more targeted fuel tanks on your way back.

MISSION 35: Operation Pegasus
STRATEGIC VALUE: 12
TAKEOFF TIME: 05:43
TAKEOFF LOCATION: Oakland International

ORDERS: Intelligence has uncovered two command bunkers and a fuel tank that seems to be supplying them. Approach the targets and destroy any air cover in the area. Then proceed to eliminate two of three ground targets. The remaining facilities will be handled by later units, *provided air cover is eliminated!*

MISSION 36: Suspected Ammo Dump
STRATEGIC VALUE: 2
TAKEOFF TIME: 03:51
TAKEOFF LOCATION: U.S.S. Constellation
ORDERS: Front-line intelligence has reported several structures holding a large cache of weapons, explosives, and command equipment (electronics gear). Target and destroy the sites while avoiding enemy air cover.

MISSION 37: Operation Christmas Lights
STRATEGIC VALUE: 12
TAKEOFF TIME: 03:40
TAKEOFF LOCATION: Oakland International
ORDERS: Two newly constructed fuel tanks have been confirmed. Target data will be downloaded to your aircraft. Destroy the targets and return to base. Avoid enemy air cover and anti-aircraft. These targets should light right up!
TACTICS: The mission orders on this one advise you to avoid contact with enemy fighters. Pay attention to this advice. The enemy fighters on this mission can be had, but they know how to go straight up and straight down and give you grief, so be careful.

MISSION 38: Operation Gopher
STRATEGIC VALUE: 14
TAKEOFF TIME: 00:21
TAKEOFF LOCATION: Oakland International
ORDERS: Reports have been floating around about a major enemy
offensive. To abort this possibility, command has decided to disable
the runways at Moffett Field to prevent the enemy from launching an
air strike this far north. Bomb the runways and return to base. Watch
for possible MiG response from San Jose.

MISSION 39: Operation Bayonet
STRATEGIC VALUE: 22
TAKEOFF TIME: 01:11
TAKEOFF LOCATION: Oakland International
ORDERS: We have selected three targets for surgical removal.
Consult on-board target information for location and heading.
Tomcat is already airborne to help take care of hostile units. Join
Tomcat after the sites are destroyed and splash a bandit.

MISSION 40: Operation Over Shoulder
STRATEGIC VALUE: 7
TAKEOFF TIME: 01:15
TAKEOFF LOCATION: U.S.S. Constellation
ORDERS: We've spotted two truck parks that should be easy
pickings for tonight. Take out at least one target. Proceed to the next
if possible. You must also engage and destroy any airborne targets.
Probability of enemy missile attack on San Francisco is high.

MISSION 41: Operation Silicon
STRATEGIC VALUE: 21
TAKEOFF TIME: 21:11
TAKEOFF LOCATION: U.S.S. Constellation
ORDERS: Several small computer manufacturing plants have been supplying electronics parts for enemy missile guidance. Destroy these targets before they can evacuate the remaining parts south. Watch for bandits in the area and destroy them if you're spotted.

MISSION 42: Operation Kill Trip
STRATEGIC VALUE: 22
TAKEOFF TIME: 02:18
TAKEOFF LOCATION: U.S.S. Constellation
ORDERS: The enemy's base at Livermore has been cut off from communications. The enemy radar net is down. Proceed to Livermore and destroy any enemy aircraft on the ground. Watch for MiG trailers on your way back; avoid them at all costs. AAA is expected to be heavy.

MISSION 43: Operation Fire Starter
STRATEGIC VALUE: 8
TAKEOFF TIME: 19:28
TAKEOFF LOCATION: U.S.S. Constellation
ORDERS: Ground forces have located three heavily armed command and control bunkers. As you know, disruption of their C and C is vital to further ops. Take out two of three targets—leave the rest for tomorrow's Hornet strikes. Try to get at least one 2000-pounder on each target. Triple-A is reported to be heavy.

MISSION 44: Operation Manifold
STRATEGIC VALUE: 10
TAKEOFF TIME: 17:07
TAKEOFF LOCATION: U.S.S. Constellation
ORDERS: Local command has selected three targets for you: a truck park, a fuel tank, and a bunker left over from a previous raid. Take out two targets before returning. Use your tactical judgment in picking targets. Avoid enemy fighter engagements. SAM activity is picking up, so watch your 6.

MISSION 45: Operation Pick-A-Mix
STRATEGIC VALUE: 11
TAKEOFF TIME: 08:27
TAKEOFF LOCATION: U.S.S. Constellation
ORDERS: We have some multi-role duty for you. Three weapons plants have been selected for destruction. Pick one of these, based on the tactical situation, and destroy it. The remaining ones will be taken out by A-6 runs. Destroy any bogeys heading toward you. Triple-A could get messy. Good luck . . . .

MISSION 46: Operation E-Z-Rider
STRATEGIC VALUE: 12
TAKEOFF TIME: 10:08
TAKEOFF LOCATION: U.S.S. Constellation
ORDERS: Two auto parts plants and one motorcycle parts plant are being used to produce bearings and machined weapons components. Strike two of three targets and report back. Use low-level interdiction to avoid enemy combat air patrols. Keep the flak off your back.
TACTICS: This is another one of those missions where it's critical that you pay attention to your mission orders. Enemy fighters, six of them, will ruin your day if you're not careful. When you bomb the targets in this mission, go for targets #1 and #2 first, using a minimum of bombs. Target #3 is difficult to see, and much harder to hit than the first two.

MISSION 47: Operation Hunker-Bunker
STRATEGIC VALUE: 20
TAKEOFF TIME: 03:18
TAKEOFF LOCATION: U.S.S. Constellation
ORDERS: There are confirmed reports of front-line command elements hunkered down in bunkers under several vacated industrial structures. Hit two of these bunkers. Try to get a 2000-pounder on each site. Expend *all* ordnance and return to the base. No Triple-A or SAM activity reported in this area, but watch out.

MISSION 48: Operation Dominion
STRATEGIC VALUE: 12
TAKEOFF TIME: 15:34
TAKEOFF LOCATION: U.S.S. Constellation
ORDERS: Two electronics plants, which were producing U.S. AAM missile parts, have been used by the enemy to enhance their SAM components. Strike both of these targets. They're poorly defended, so use multiple 500-lb bombs and flatten both structures. Enemy CAP is your area. Avoid air-to-air engagement at all costs.
TACTICS: Avoid enemy aircraft on this mission. In fact, on this mission you can ignore enemy fighters and fly right past them. Pull in your fangs here, because if you can't resist the urge to engage the enemy on this mission you'll end up walking to your targets.

MISSION 49: Operation Magnum
STRATEGIC VALUE: 18
TAKEOFF TIME: 05:44
TAKEOFF LOCATION: U.S.S. Constellation
ORDERS: More weapons storage facilities have been located. Two *important* targets have been downloaded to your aircraft. Hit both of them with all available munitions. Avoid debris from secondary explosions. Expect heavy flak in the area. Best bailout to the west. Good hunting!

MISSION 50: Operation Bandit Base
STRATEGIC VALUE: 15
TAKEOFF TIME: 04:44
TAKEOFF LOCATION: U.S.S. Constellation
ORDERS: Tactical intelligence reports several enemy aircraft refueling at Moffett Field. Destroy at least two aircraft on the ground. If any manage to get airborne, engage and destroy. A commando squad will be sent to destroy any remaining enemy airplanes at Moffett. We're not sure whether any Triple-A remains, so be careful.
TACTICS: Attacking enemy airfields is an important part of the OCA campaign, but these missions are always high-risk. After takeoff, turn to a heading of 130 degrees and descend to low altitude before you get to the Bay Area. This will delay detection by enemy

acquisition systems. Airfields are usually defended by AAA, SAMs, and an airborne CAP (combat air patrol), so heads up! If there is a CAP near the airfield, ambush and kill it. Remember that you're flying an LO aircraft armed with AMRAAMs. After engaging and destroying the CAP, you can attack the aircraft on the runways. Aircraft on the ground are good targets for KEM and 20-mm. If air defenses are light, you can hone your rocket and strafe attack skills.

MISSION 51: 757 In Danger!
STRATEGIC VALUE: 14
TAKEOFF TIME: 12:53
TAKEOFF LOCATION: U.S.S. Constellation
ORDERS: Scramble immediately to intercept a group of targets that appear to be intercepting a friendly transport aircraft. Protect the aircraft at all costs. Knock out at least two hostile aircraft in the area. Backup units will clean up any stragglers.
TACTICS: The fight is very close to you on this mission. After you launch from the carrier, the target that is closest to your jet is the 757. In order to protect it, go to AB and commit on the closest target to the 757. This mission is very similar to a real-world DCA mission, such as protecting the AWACS or JSTARS aircraft. When these real-world high-value assets come under attack, the fighter pilot's job is to immediately engage the attacking enemy fighters while the big aircraft retrogrades (runs). This mission is pretty much the same. Go full-speed to the merge with the enemy, but fly a stern conversion if possible. Once you arrive in the bandit's 6 o'clock, control your airspeed so you don't overshoot the target.

MISSION 52: How 'Bout a Night CAP
STRATEGIC VALUE: 5
TAKEOFF TIME: 22:04
TAKEOFF LOCATION: Moffett Field
ORDERS: Take off and tangle with enemy Combat Air Patrol flying night cover. They've been flying overconfidently lately, so let's give them a bloody nose and show them who's boss. Watch for Triple-A on your way to intercept. Send three bogeys into the sea tonight. Good hunting!

MISSION 53: Move on Moffett
STRATEGIC VALUE: 15
TAKEOFF TIME: 07:57
TAKEOFF LOCATION: U.S.S. Constellation
ORDERS: We have launch confirmation of two Cruise missiles. Preliminary data suggest they may be headed toward Moffett Field. If they score, this could really slow down rear theater supply efforts. Intercept and destroy missiles, and any enemy fighter cover with them. Ground crews at Moffett are counting on you.

MISSION 54: Carrier Cover
STRATEGIC VALUE: 13
TAKEOFF TIME: 22:30
TAKEOFF LOCATION: U.S.S. Constellation
ORDERS: Hawkeyes and AWACS confirm multiple inbound targets. Launch and engage as far away from the carrier as possible. Expect and react to any anti-ship missile launches. Remember, your job is to save the carrier. Splash bogeys and any missiles they may launch. Get out there!
TACTICS: On this mission you have to sort the incoming targets quickly and get to the merge as fast as possible. When you arrive at the merge, watch your overtake.

MISSION 55: Missile Mayhem
STRATEGIC VALUE: 13
TAKEOFF TIME: 18:37
TAKEOFF LOCATION: Moffett Field
ORDERS: Two inbound Cruise missiles are being tracked. Intercept immediately to splash these threats. We don't like to rely on our close-in anti-missile systems if we don't have to. Expect fighter trailers to give you trouble. Splash anything that doesn't speak English. Take care up there!
TACTICS: This mission is a tough one. The enemy is using anti-sort tactics to hide their Exocet or Cruise missiles. Their anti-sort tactics on this mission consist of splitting the attackers into two groups, or entities. A group is a formation of fighters that are within 3 miles of each other. Within the group there are two targets. One of these is a Cruise or Exocet missile. The object here is to sort the groups using the Map view and then target the nearest group (which is the greatest

threat) to the ship. Once you're flying toward this near group, you must now sort within the group to find the Cruise or Exocet missile. Once you find the high-threat target within the group, you should blast it first and then engage the fighter that's flying with it. Don't get tied up for too long, because the other group is still a threat. After destroying the near group, use the Map view to start your intercept on the far group. Again, sort within the group to find the high-threat target. On this mission all targets must be destroyed.

MISSION 56: Even Odds
STRATEGIC VALUE: 6
TAKEOFF TIME: 21:03
TAKEOFF LOCATION: U.S.S. Constellation
ORDERS: AWACS are reporting three bogeys airborne. Two appear to be headed south, but the third is approaching fast. Launch and engage inbound bogey at greatest possible distance. He could be carrying Exocet missiles. Splash him before any launch is possible.

MISSION 57: Midnight Furball
STRATEGIC VALUE: 13
TAKEOFF TIME: 0:13
TAKEOFF LOCATION: U.S.S. Constellation
ORDERS: Quite a morning! We have three bandits inbound looking for trouble, so let's get out there and give it to them. Looks like several SU-27s, so be alert. Triple-A expected to be light. We'll be watching the fireworks from here. Give us a good show!
TACTICS: After launch from the carrier, come to a heading of 125 degrees to close with your targets. This mission is a One versus Three fight, so somebody has to go to the meat locker at the merge or the fight will be suicide. The best way to approach this merge is the same way you should approach any fight in an LO aircraft. Stay in LO mode as long as possible and run a stern conversion on the enemy formation. Launch an AMRAAM when you're in range. If you don't kill a bandit coming into the fight, blow through at full AB and run away. When you get about 20 miles from the fight, turn back and try the intercept and AMRAAM attack again. Remember, before mixing it up in a sustained turning engagement you should kill one of the bandits. Even if you're down to a One versus Two and things aren't going well, you can separate from the fight and come back in again.

MISSION 58: Operation Avalanche
STRATEGIC VALUE: 15
TAKEOFF TIME: 12:30
TAKEOFF LOCATION: U.S.S. Constellation
ORDERS: Intelligence has targeted three weapons facilities for destruction. Scramble immediately for precision bombing run. Intercept and engage any hostile interceptors. SAM sightings are high. Consult avionics data for target heading and distance. Clear skies with fair visibility. Winds out of the south at 20 knots. MiGs reported on patrol.

MISSION 59: Operation Overlord
STRATEGIC VALUE: 15
TAKEOFF TIME: 12:30
TAKEOFF LOCATION: U.S.S. Constellation
ORDERS: You need to hit two of three weapons complexes on this strike. The enemy is using these factories to supply their ground weapons with spare parts. You also have to take out any bandits which head your way. Try to hit your targets early to lighten your load. Good luck—this could get messy.

MISSION 60: Operation Onslaught
STRATEGIC VALUE: 14
TAKEOFF TIME: 12:23
TAKEOFF LOCATION: U.S.S. Constellation
ORDERS: Three groups of trucks have been lined up to receive some punishment today. Get out there and pound 'em hard. Expect anti-air assets to be in full use. Enemy fighter cover is bound to be active, but try to avoid engagement if possible. These trucks are important targets, so don't get yourself shot down.
TACTICS: On this mission you're advised to avoid engagement with enemy aircraft. The best way to avoid a fight is to use speed to get to your ground targets fast and destroy them. A low-altitude level bomb pass will be effective, but don't slow down until you're 10 miles from the target. If you miss the target, do not re-attack. A re-attack will give pursuing enemy fighters a cut-off vector as you swing around for another pass. If you miss the first target, accelerate at full AB and go to the next target. After bombing the targets, you can engage and kill the enemy aircraft. Fly a stern conversion if possible and use AMRAAMS.

MISSION 61: Operation Sweep Up
STRATEGIC VALUE: 12
TAKEOFF TIME: 04:28
TAKEOFF LOCATION: Moffett Field
ORDERS: Central Command has given us three targets. Destroying them will be part of battlefield cleanup operations. Two fuel storage facilities and a truck park area need to be taken out to secure this battlefield once and for all. Take out all three targets while avoiding enemy fighter patrols. Watch for low-level Triple-A.

MISSION 62: Operation First Light
STRATEGIC VALUE: 11
TAKEOFF TIME: 04:15
TAKEOFF LOCATION: U.S.S. Constellation
ORDERS: Good morning, gentlemen! We have a group of targets for you to take out bright and early before the sun comes up. Take out two primary targets: a lightly fortified command structure and a tank being used for jet fuel. Proceed to third target if tactical situation permits. Engage any interceptors that track you.

MISSION 63: Operation Powderkeg
STRATEGIC VALUE: 21
TAKEOFF TIME: 12:41
TAKEOFF LOCATION: U.S.S. Constellation
ORDERS: We've got two ammunition storage facilities to light up today. Move in low and put a heavy bomb on each to weaken any reinforcement they may have built. Proceed to third target if tactical situation permits. Avoid enemy air patrols if at all possible.

MISSION 64: Supply Strangle
STRATEGIC VALUE: 12
TAKEOFF TIME: 3:17
TAKEOFF LOCATION: Moffett Field
ORDERS: We need to move in and take care of some supply trucks. Take out both primary truck convoys and proceed to secondary target if tactical situation permits. Engage any bogeys that track you. Watch for SAM activity during bomb runs.

MISSION 65: Boss the Bandits
STRATEGIC VALUE: 7
TAKEOFF TIME: 05:31
TAKEOFF LOCATION: U.S.S. Constellation
ORDERS: Three mid-priority targets have presented themselves: two ammo dumps and a jet fuel tank. Since you'll also have to engage any enemy fighters, CentCom is only requiring you to take out one target. Get rid of your bombs fast and wax those bandits. Go out and show them who's the boss up there.

MISSION 66: Operation Midnight Convoy
STRATEGIC VALUE: 10
TAKEOFF TIME: 23:18
TAKEOFF LOCATION: U.S.S. Constellation
ORDERS: The enemy is getting bold—it seems to have regulated its midnight air convoy out of Salinas. Well, tonight we'll be ready. Launch and intercept convoy. Splash all transports. If enemy fighters engage, feel free to go after them instead. Then take out transports if possible. Expect anti-air assets to be in use on approach.

MISSION 67: Operation Tito
STRATEGIC VALUE: 14
TAKEOFF TIME: 13:10
TAKEOFF LOCATION: U.S.S. Constellation
ORDERS: We need to set some fuel on fire today. We're going to catch it for all the smoke, but this should seriously hamper their long-term CAP ability. Watch for enemy fighters and engage any interceptors that get interested in your activities. Flak and SAM activity questionable.
TACTICS: It's best to approach the target at low altitude on this mission. Go in fast and low (500 feet or lower) to avoid contact with enemy fighters. Hit the target with your bombs, then engage the enemy aircraft.

MISSION 68: Operation Ram
STRATEGIC VALUE: 9
TAKEOFF TIME: 21:23
TAKEOFF LOCATION: U.S.S. Constellation
ORDERS: We've really lucked out this time! Civilian spotters report

three enemy fighters on the ground near Salinas. They haven't moved in 3 days and are probably waiting for spare parts. Blow them up before the enemy can use them. Watch for local anti-aircraft.

TACTICS: On this mission, if you encounter enemy aircraft flying a CAP, engage and destroy them before you hit your ground targets. The ground targets are parked aircraft, and you can see them and hit them better if you use a low-altitude level bomb pass.

MISSION 69: Operation Drumbeat
STRATEGIC VALUE: 2
TAKEOFF TIME: 09:53
TAKEOFF LOCATION: U.S.S. Constellation
ORDERS: Civilian informers have passed information to us about three enemy command posts stationed under several buildings in this sector. These posts probably serve as a vital communications link to the south. Hit these targets hard—try to bring down the structures. Avoid enemy CAP if at all possible.

MISSION 70: Operation Chieftain
STRATEGIC VALUE: 4
TAKEOFF TIME: 20:35
TAKEOFF LOCATION: U.S.S. Constellation
ORDERS: Scramble immediately to target and destroy two of three command bunkers listed in your ground target avionics. You'll probably need to sit a 2000-pounder on each bunker. Intercept any bogeys that may be tailing you. Proceed to third target if tactical situation permits.

TACTICS: On this mission either 500-pound Mark-82s or 2000-pound Mark-84s will destroy the targets. After you hit the target, shoot down the enemy aircraft in the CAP.

MISSION 71: Operation Triumph
STRATEGIC VALUE: 13
TAKEOFF TIME: 08:37
TAKEOFF LOCATION: U.S.S. Constellation
ORDERS: Take out two primary targets—truck parking facilities— and proceed to the third if possible. We expect enemy fighter patrols to be alerted to your presence, since enemy radar activity has picked up. Avoid fighter cover if possible and return to base after destroying the primary targets. Expect moderate anti-air activity.

MISSION 72: Operation Crusher
STRATEGIC VALUE: 12
TAKEOFF TIME: 07:25
TAKEOFF LOCATION: U.S.S. Constellation
ORDERS: We have targeted two warehouses converted into weapons production plants. Take out these plants, then move on to flatten a local fuel tank. Watch out for large secondary explosions. Avoid enemy air patrols if possible. You'll be in broad daylight, so keep your eyes open. Good luck and good shooting!

MISSION 73: Operation Pop Top
STRATEGIC VALUE: 22
TAKEOFF TIME: 14:17
TAKEOFF LOCATION: U.S.S. Constellation
ORDERS: There are trucks everywhere. Take out the first two targets—truck convoys— with appropriate weapons. Then seek out and engage any enemy air patrols in your area. We're sending in unescorted A-6 strikes later and can't afford to lose them to MiGs. Watch out below for SAM and Triple-A activity. Good luck!

MISSION 74: Operation Landfill
STRATEGIC VALUE: 12
TAKEOFF TIME: 00:47
TAKEOFF LOCATION: U.S.S. Constellation
ORDERS: We have three bunkers that need to be taken out. We expect high-ranking enemy officers to be inside them. Use all your ordnance and cave those suckers in. If you're spotted by bogeys, engage and destroy. This is an important mission, so be careful and watch your 6.

MISSION 75: Backyard Bar-B-Que
STRATEGIC VALUE: 14
TAKEOFF TIME: 22:23
TAKEOFF LOCATION: U.S.S. Constellation
ORDERS: Intelligence has some hot spots for you to take care of tonight. Two fuel tanks and a munitions storage facility are just waiting to be lit up. Mission planners recommend a high-altitude attack to avoid possible large secondary explosions. We expect enemy air cover to be in place, but avoid engagement if at all possible.

MISSION 76: Missile Mania
STRATEGIC VALUE: 12
TAKEOFF TIME: 22:10
TAKEOFF LOCATION: U.S.S. Constellation
ORDERS: Scramble immediately to intercept and splash two inbound Cruise missiles. Watch for MiG cover. They're used to our anti-Cruise missile tactics. Take out any fighters you encounter.

MISSION 77: Wounded Ducks
STRATEGIC VALUE: 11
TAKEOFF TIME: 03:06
TAKEOFF LOCATION: U.S.S. Constellation
ORDERS: AWACS have spotted four—correction five—bogeys heading toward the carrier. Intercept immediately. We recently destroyed a munitions plant, which has probably decreased the arms they're carrying, so play it safe and wear them down. Take out four of five bandits.

MISSION 78: AFT Down!
STRATEGIC VALUE: 19
TAKEOFF TIME: 07:52
TAKEOFF LOCATION: U.S.S. Constellation
ORDERS: We have a crisis situation. A friendly F-23 has gone down behind enemy lines. The pilot is reported to be alive and making his way to safety via the California underground, but his aircraft is intact and on the ground. Locate and destroy any remains of this ATF. MiGs are converging on it—don't let them beat you to it!
TACTICS: This is a critical mission. Your best bet is to fly the ATF on this mission, since the CAP over the target area will be heavy. Take off and turn to an initial heading of 093 degrees. As you approach the target area, you'll start to encounter the CAP. Run an LO stern conversion on these targets and engage and kill them one by one. This is another One versus Three fight, so shoot as soon as you're in weapons parameters to kill the bandit and even the odds. On this mission it's generally better to take out all three aircraft in the CAP before bombing the ATF crash site. You can go straight for the site, but if you do, you better go fast and use your countermeasures.

MISSION 79: Missile Madness
STRATEGIC VALUE: 12
TAKEOFF TIME: 11:27
TAKEOFF LOCATION: U.S.S. Constellation
ORDERS: Looks like another missile launch on the carrier. Scramble immediately to intercept two suspected Cruise missiles targeted for our boat. Expect enemy fighters to be covering their inbound birds. Engage and destroy any fighters that move on you. Let's get out there!

MISSION 80: Furball Frenzy
STRATEGIC VALUE: 12
TAKEOFF TIME: 07:48
TAKEOFF LOCATION: U.S.S. Constellation
ORDERS: Launch immediately to intercept and engage hostile interceptors headed this way. Intelligence suggests these bandits may be some of the enemy's better pilots. Watch your 6 and don't overextend. We can't afford to lose you now! Splash at least three bogeys and return. Expect heavy air cover inbound to interception.

MISSION 81: Carrier Under Siege
STRATEGIC VALUE: 20
TAKEOFF TIME: 07:47
TAKEOFF LOCATION: U.S.S. Constellation
ORDERS: *Alert!* Two incoming Cruise missiles targeting the carrier. Two MiGs flying air cover to draw fire from missiles. F-18s on maneuvers, Tomcat patrols out of range and low on fuel. You have to defend the ship. Splash all bogeys. We're counting on you!
TACTICS: We've already discussed these scenarios in detail. This one is no different from the others. Take off and turn to a heading of 090 degrees to close with the targets. Perform a good sort so you're sure that you're running on the Cruise missiles first. On this mission SAMs will be a factor, so use your countermeasures when necessary.

MISSION 82: Vandenberg Attack
STRATEGIC VALUE: 19
TAKEOFF TIME: 12:15
TAKEOFF LOCATION: U.S.S. Constellation
ORDERS: AWACS and ground radar confirm three inbound Cruise missiles targeted for Vandenberg AFB. Intercept and destroy missiles before they hit the airbase. Watch for MiG cover, but concentrate on the missiles. Lives are at stake!

MISSION 83: Operation Shatter
STRATEGIC VALUE: 20
TAKEOFF TIME: 04:03
TAKEOFF LOCATION: U.S.S. Constellation
ORDERS: Our ground forces have pinned down three vital targets that you must destroy before enemy reinforcements arrive. Use *extreme* caution to avoid collateral friendly losses. Enemy fighter harassment is *expected*. Take out at least one bandit after your successful target strikes.

MISSION 84: Operation Anvil
STRATEGIC VALUE: 18
TAKEOFF TIME: 03:13
TAKEOFF LOCATION: U.S.S. Constellation
ORDERS: Locate and destroy two small convoys of trucks hauling military goods into enemy areas. Last known position downloaded to aircraft. Engage and destroy any enemy combat air patrol that may spot you. Watch for heavy Triple-A on your way in and coming back. Good hunting!

MISSION 85: Operation Iron Eagle
STRATEGIC VALUE: 15
TAKEOFF TIME: 13:03
TAKEOFF LOCATION: U.S.S. Constellation
ORDERS: Two fuel tanks are ripe for the attack. We have also located a small command bunker as a secondary target. Take out tanks and secondary target if possible. Also engage and destroy one enemy combat air patrol unit. Watch for others in the area. SAM and Triple-A reported normal. Good shooting. . . .

MISSION 86: Suspected Parts Convoy
STRATEGIC VALUE: 5
TAKEOFF TIME: 04:08
TAKEOFF LOCATION: U.S.S. Constellation
ORDERS: Behind-the-lines intelligence sources indicate that a small group of trucks may be carrying parts *vital* to enemy air transport capabilities. Hit this primary target and two secondaries. Engage any hostile aircraft that may be alerted to your presence. Watch for SAM activity inbound to targets.

MISSION 87: Operation Waspnest
STRATEGIC VALUE: 12
TAKEOFF TIME: 10:38
TAKEOFF LOCATION: U.S.S. Constellation
ORDERS: Attack and destroy convoy of three enemy air transports, probably Il-96 types. Aircraft are heading southeast, trying to evacuate parts and supplies from Ventura. Be cautious! These aircraft will probably be leading you into a real waspnest of bandits. Destroy enemy fighters if possible. Good luck !

MISSION 88: Operation Battle Ax
STRATEGIC VALUE: 16
TAKEOFF TIME: 00:03
TAKEOFF LOCATION: U.S.S. Constellation
ORDERS: We need you to stomp on two truck parks to prevent movement of troop supplies. If trouble arises, proceed to secondary target, a jet fuel storage facility. Important: due to frequent Cruise missile launches, you *must* ID any bogeys in the area and destroy any Cruise missiles.

MISSION 89: Operation Frostbite
STRATEGIC VALUE: 17
TAKEOFF TIME: 10:43
TAKEOFF LOCATION: U.S.S. Constellation
ORDERS: Long-term IR imaging has detected several facilities producing and storing liquid nitrogen, used in cooling enemy aircraft avionics. This could be one of their only sources for this vital element. Knock out both targets and return to base. Watch for heavy Triple-A and enemy CAP.

MISSION 90: Operation Bulletshot
STRATEGIC VALUE: 25
TAKEOFF TIME: 22:36
TAKEOFF LOCATION: U.S.S. Constellation
ORDERS: Rough duty ahead. We need you to take out the primary target, a fuel tank, ASAP. The enemy is drawing heavily on this resource. You must also engage and destroy an enemy fighter patrol of two bandits. You're the only one available to keep them from harassing our ground troops.
TACTICS: This is a very typical JetFighter mission, except for its high strategic value. Take out the enemy fighter CAP before bombing the target.

MISSION 91: Operation Compass
STRATEGIC VALUE: 5
TAKEOFF TIME: 18:28
TAKEOFF LOCATION: U.S.S. Constellation
ORDERS: The target list has been downloaded to your aircraft. All sites are *high* priority for degrading their ability to wage a ground campaign. We have reason to believe that enemy CAP will be heavy, and their radar net may be active again, so avoid hostile air encounters if possible. Good luck and good shooting!

MISSION 92: Operation Citadel
STRATEGIC VALUE: 12
TAKEOFF TIME: 18:23
TAKEOFF LOCATION: U.S.S. Constellation
ORDERS: Intelligence has supplied us with three mid-level targets. Destroy at least two targets and proceed to the third, if the situation permits. Select targets using your own tactical judgment. Engage and destroy any hostile targets that spot you. Enemy radar network is in questionable condition, but proceed with caution.

MISSION 93: Operation Siphon
STRATEGIC VALUE: 8
TAKEOFF TIME: 09:14
TAKEOFF LOCATION: U.S.S. Constellation
ORDERS: Two hardened command bunkers have been located in fallout shelters under two local buildings. Hit each with a 2000 lb bomb and use remaining munitions to level any above-ground structures. These are major units of their southern command and control structure. Engage and destroy any fighter patrols.

MISSION 94: Operation Gomorrah
STRATEGIC VALUE: 22
TAKEOFF TIME: 04:53
TAKEOFF LOCATION: U.S.S. Constellation
ORDERS: Two minor command bunkers need to be taken out after the destruction of a large munitions cache. Consult your avionics for target distance and heading. Keep an eye out for high-altitude enemy fighter cover. Anti-air expected to be average.

MISSION 95: Operation Juggler
STRATEGIC VALUE: 7
TAKEOFF TIME: 04:41
TAKEOFF LOCATION: U.S.S. Constellation
ORDERS: The commander of ground forces requests that three targets—two truck parks and their related ammo dump—be taken out in support of a pending allied troop movement. Destroy *at least* two of these targets and take out any low-altitude bandits that may be flying close air support.

MISSION 96: Operation Counterblow
STRATEGIC VALUE: 15
TAKEOFF TIME: 05:55
TAKEOFF LOCATION: U.S.S.Constellation
ORDERS: Intelligence has targeted a weapons plant for destruction. Scramble immediately for precision bombing run and take out two of three targets. Intercept and engage any hostile interceptors. Consult avionics data for target heading and distance. Clear skies with fair visibility. Winds out of the south at 20 knots. MiGs reported on patrol.

MISSION 97: Operation Molehill
STRATEGIC VALUE: 22
TAKEOFF TIME: 00:17
TAKEOFF LOCATION: U.S.S. Constellation
ORDERS:We've got some more truck-flattening lined up for tonight! Head out under cover of darkness and attack two truck parks. Save some munitions for target #3, a fuel tank. A pair of bandits is expected to be patrolling. Engage and destroy at least one. Tomcat will be launched to engage remaining aircraft.

MISSION 98: Operation Torch
STRATEGIC VALUE: 16
TAKEOFF TIME: 09:38
TAKEOFF LOCATION: U.S.S. Constellation
ORDERS: Central Command has given us three low-priority targets. Select one as tactical situation permits. Destruction of enemy air units, however, is crucial. Intercept and destroy *any* enemy aircraft in the region. Our ground forces are counting on you.

MISSION 99: Operation Hornet
STRATEGIC VALUE: 15
TAKEOFF TIME: 02:00
TAKEOFF LOCATION: U.S.S. Constellation
ORDERS: To avoid possible high losses of Special Forces units, CentCom has asked us to hit three mid-level command bunkers. This should seriously hamper their command and control capabilities in the area. Avoid enemy fighter engagements if possible. Anti-air assets questionable.

MISSION 100: Missile Attack
STRATEGIC VALUE: 13
TAKEOFF TIME: 14:19
TAKEOFF LOCATION: U.S.S. Constellation
ORDERS: Locate and destroy a small convoy of trucks that have been providing resupply to ground forces. Keep your eyes open for missile launches. Recent activity suggests that their guided missile capability may be back on-line. Intercept and destroy *any* enemy missiles.

MISSION 101: Fleet Defense (Ugh!)
STRATEGIC VALUE: 25
TAKEOFF TIME: 03:06
TAKEOFF LOCATION: U.S.S. Constellation
ORDERS: Fleet defense is tracking multiple targets inbound. Could be a large-scale air attack on the carrier. Splash *any* hostile craft in our airspace. Consult AWACS download for up-to-date target information. Pack your chute carefully. This is what the F-14 was built for!
TACTICS: This is one of the hardest fleet defense missions, so you may want to fly the F-14. This aircraft can carry a large air-to-air fleet defense load, and you're going to need it. After launch from the carrier, turn to 072 degrees to intercept the closest target, which is a group carrying four Exocet missiles. The best tactic is to knock out these targets fast with all available resources, then return to the carrier to re-arm. This group of Exocets will hit the carrier very fast if you don't close and destroy them. Once you destroy this group, you have time before the next group gets close to the ship. After launching the second time from the ship, use the Map view to find the next closest group and attack it. On this mission you have to sweep the sky clear of all bandits. Be careful not to waste your missile on this mission.

MISSION 102: Three Missiles
STRATEGIC VALUE: 24
TAKEOFF TIME: 09:52
TAKEOFF LOCATION: U.S.S.Constellation
ORDERS: AEGIS confirms multiple missile launches directed toward carrier. Scramble immediately to intercept and destroy missiles. Phalanx turrets two and three currently inoperative. Watch out for MiG cover. We're counting on you.

TACTICS: Tense! One Cruise missile is high; the other two are low. Get the high one first. Ignore the SU-27 and chaff any SAMs that lock onto you. Keep things interesting by playing surgeon, and use only one Sidewinder per Cruise missile.

MISSION 103: Patrol in San Juan Canyon
STRATEGIC VALUE: 5
TAKEOFF TIME: 12:01
TAKEOFF LOCATION: U.S.S. Constellation
ORDERS: Take off immediately and join with Tomcat 1. Four bogeys of unknown type patrolling in San Juan Canyon. Intercept and destroy ASAP.

MISSION 104: Three on Me
STRATEGIC VALUE: 11
TAKEOFF TIME: 15:12
TAKEOFF LOCATION: U.S.S. Constellation
ORDERS: Scramble immediately to intercept and destroy three inbound targets. Types unknown, but speed and flight characteristics indicate modern fighter craft. Expect SAM firings even with enemy aircraft present.

MISSION 105: Missile Attack
STRATEGIC VALUE: 11
TAKEOFF TIME: 00:45
TAKEOFF LOCATION: U.S.S. Constellation
ORDERS: Cruise missiles reported launched from south of L.A. Intercept and destroy. Enemy combat air patrols are sure to be waiting for our response, but your first priority is downing those missiles. Good luck—you'll need it!

MISSION 106: Hornet SOS!
STRATEGIC VALUE: 5
TAKEOFF TIME: 09:17
TAKEOFF LOCATION: U.S.S. Constellation
ORDERS: Two F-18s are in trouble. Hornets low on fuel and arms have flown into a patrol of MiGs. Get out there and help the Hornet pilots.

MISSION 107: Furball from Palm Springs
STRATEGIC VALUE: 11
TAKEOFF TIME: 06:58
TAKEOFF LOCATION: U.S.S. Constellation
ORDERS: What a mess! We don't know where they scraped these up, but there are five MiGs inbound. Observers say they're armed for air-to-air. Splash at least three bandits.

MISSION 108: Missile Barrage
STRATEGIC VALUE: 18
TAKEOFF TIME: 11:30
TAKEOFF LOCATION: U.S.S. Constellation
ORDERS: The Cruise missile launch we expected has finally occurred. We have an F-18 heading for interception. Join Hornet and splash all inbound targets.
TACTICS: This mission can get confusing. Remember to sort the targets and close with the Cruise missiles first.

MISSION 109: Operation Glass Eye
STRATEGIC VALUE: 10
TAKEOFF TIME: 05:36
TAKEOFF LOCATION: U.S.S. Constellation
ORDERS: A weapons plant complex is stepping up production of radar-seeking missile parts. We have to destroy this complex and keep the enemy's munitions supplies low. You'll be joined by an F-14 flying patrol in the area. Watch for bogeys.

MISSION 110: Operation Broadside
STRATEGIC VALUE: 10
TAKEOFF TIME: 05:36
TAKEOFF LOCATION: U.S.S. Constellation
ORDERS: Intelligence reports confirm a group of suspected munitions storage camps. We've got them on the run already—knock out this cache and they'll have a hard time getting another ground assault together. Keep an eye out for bandits and heavy flak.

MISSION 111: Operation Beartrap
STRATEGIC VALUE: 10
TAKEOFF TIME: 05:36
TAKEOFF LOCATION: U.S.S. Constellation
ORDERS: A small but important fuel depot has been supplying front-line forces. Take out this depot and the transport trucks that just left it. On your return flight, destroy munitions cache if weapons are available, but be aware of heavy enemy fighter cover.

MISSION 112: Operation Big Bang
STRATEGIC VALUE: 20
TAKEOFF TIME: 07:37
TAKEOFF LOCATION: U.S.S. Constellation
ORDERS: Mid-level tactical targets must be blasted to cut enemy supply lines. Take out all three targets. Check aircraft display for target heading and distance. We sent in an F-16 to do the job, but we've lost contact. If you establish contact, assist immediately, then wax targets.

MISSION 113: Suspected Truck Park
STRATEGIC VALUE: 2
TAKEOFF TIME: 04:06
TAKEOFF LOCATION: U.S.S. Constellation
ORDERS: Intelligence reports a small probability of a truck park full of important technical supplies for enemy aircraft. If it's there and you take it out, you could set back enemy aircraft repair by 2 weeks. If not—oh, well.

MISSION 114: Operation Blacktop
STRATEGIC VALUE: 7
TAKEOFF TIME: 15:24
TAKEOFF LOCATION: U.S.S. Constellation
ORDERS: SAC demands a strike on LAX to cut off transport landings. The airfield is buzzing with fighters and brimming with SAM sites. Join Hornet and take out both targets and one bandit between you. Best of luck—you'll need it!
TACTICS: A friendly F/A-18 is out in front of you and to your left at the start of this mission. Disregard it and head for the target area. If you encounter an enemy CAP on the way to the target area, engage and destroy it. On this mission the enemy has placed two CAPs in your path, so don't waste missiles.

MISSION 115: Operation Nightstalk
STRATEGIC VALUE: 15
TAKEOFF TIME: 01:55
TAKEOFF LOCATION: U.S.S. Constellation
ORDERS: Three weapons storage facilities have been highly active in the past few days. We believe they're receiving munitions from previously damaged structures. Approach and attack *all* targets. Enemy CAP is heavy, so conceal yourself during approach. SAM and Triple-A are nightmarish. Fly low and hit hard.

MISSION 116: Operation Rat's Den
STRATEGIC VALUE: 15
TAKEOFF TIME: 05:37
TAKEOFF LOCATION: U.S.S. Constellation
ORDERS: We're seeing a lot more enemy aircraft than we'd like to. That's why we've targeted two fuel tanks and a parts depot to be flattened. This is a high-risk operation, and we believe the enemy expects it, but the job has to be done. Hit all targets and take out any bandits that spot you. Good luck!

MISSION 117: Operation Shellgame
STRATEGIC VALUE: 10
TAKEOFF TIME: 19:16
TAKEOFF LOCATION: U.S.S. Constellation
ORDERS: We've been tracking several trucks containing important spares for the SU-27. Find and destroy these trucks. Their last location has been downloaded to your aircraft. Drop the rest of your munitions on two fuel tanks in the area. Engage any enemy aircraft that come after you. Heavy Triple-A reported.

MISSION 118: Operation Hide 'n' Seek
STRATEGIC VALUE: 6
TAKEOFF TIME: 07:09
TAKEOFF LOCATION: U.S.S. Constellation
ORDERS: Remaining SU-27 spare parts have been hidden in several depots in the area. We need to hit all three targets and hit them soon! Combat Air Patrol has its hands full, so help out with the bogeys after your drop. Take out two bandits between you and the allied Hornet in the area. Good luck!

MISSION 119: Operation Puzzle
STRATEGIC VALUE: 20
TAKEOFF TIME: 14:51
TAKEOFF LOCATION: U.S.S. Constellation
ORDERS: To tell the truth, we don't know what's being moved between these three targets, but there's a lot of it. Intelligence suggests highly sensitive materials. After target destruction, assist allied F/A-18 and splash bandit if he hasn't been splashed already. Good hunting!

MISSION 120: Multi-Role Maelstrom
STRATEGIC VALUE: 25
TAKEOFF TIME: 21:13
TAKEOFF LOCATION: U.S.S. Constellation
ORDERS: We absolutely need these three targets flattened—they have high strategic importance. Enemy CAP is heavy, and may be aware of the urgency of this operation. You'll need to engage and destroy enemy aircraft as well. Pack your chute carefully—this one's going to be tough.

MISSION 121: Operation Scout
STRATEGIC VALUE: 12
TAKEOFF TIME: 05:13
TAKEOFF LOCATION: U.S.S. Constellation
ORDERS: We have three targets lined up for today. They need to be hit, but almost more important, your sight camera footage will undergo heavy analysis to determine condition of personnel. Scout 'em out, blow 'em up, and get home safe! Enemy is flying CAP at Angels 30, so keep looking over your shoulder.

MISSION 122: Final Offensive
STRATEGIC VALUE: 25
TAKEOFF TIME: 01:26
TAKEOFF LOCATION: U.S.S. Constellation
ORDERS: We've located the largest remaining enemy ammo dumps. Intelligence suggests that they're lightly armored, so watch out for large secondaries as you pull out. After you hit the targets, assist Tomcat 1 if necessary. This could seal the enemy's fate. Good luck!

MISSION 123: Operation Convergence
STRATEGIC VALUE: 25
TAKEOFF TIME: 04:13
TAKEOFF LOCATION: U.S.S. Constellation
ORDERS: Three targets downloaded to aircraft: two depots and a fuel tank. Hit 'em hard and fast. The enemy radar net may be intermittently active, so keep an eye out for CAP converging on your location. Engage and destroy any targets that find you. We're winning already, but let's seal it up!

MISSION 124: Operation Clean Sweep
STRATEGIC VALUE: 25
TAKEOFF TIME: 02:57
TAKEOFF LOCATION: U.S.S. Constellation
ORDERS: We've detected a group of active chemical facilities that may be producing an agent that's deliverable in artillery shells. Destroy all targets and return to base. Enemy CAP is moderate, but their radar net may be up again, so keep your eyes open.
TACTICS: This mission has one of the highest strategic values in the

game, so remember the basics. Fly low and stay in LO mode as long as possible to avoid detection by the enemy. If you do get engaged by enemy fighters, use AMRAAMs to kill them fast.

MISSION 125: Convoy Killer
STRATEGIC VALUE: 23
TAKEOFF TIME: 19:53
TAKEOFF LOCATION: U.S.S. Constellation
ORDERS: Intercept and destroy a convoy of Il-96 transport aircraft heading south. You'll have to approach full-AB and engage before they escape to the south. Watch for escorts. Splash all five transports, or, if possible, take out the bogeys *and* the transports. If you succeed, this will put a big dent in the enemy's ability to wage war in the future.
TACTICS: When you go after slow movers with an escort, you always have to take out the escort first. On this mission the Il-96s have fighter escort, so ignore the transports as you come into the fight and shoot down the enemy fighters using a stern conversion. After you splash the escort, you can take your time with the transports.

A Appendix: Questions and Answers

This section deals with some of the more common questions people ask about playing JetFighter II. If you don't find your question here, check the next section, "Technical Questions and Answers." It has more detailed information about problems you may encounter when you run JetFighter II on your computer.

Q: How do I get the ILS to point to a different airport if I want to land there to refuel?

A: JetFighter II doesn't have that ability. What you should do is go into Free Flight and land at the various airports. Make a note of the latitude and longitude of each.

Q: How do I use the KEMs?

A: The Kinetic Energy Missiles can be thought of as something between a missile and a cannon. They're laser-guided, but can only fly straight. This means they don't have the parabolic flight path that cannon rounds do. They are *not* radar-guided to follow their target. To use the KEM, select it as your weapon, line up your target, and fire. You won't see the missile seeker, because the KEM is not a "smart" missile. A burst of two or three helps increase your coverage and improves your chance of a hit. Unlike a cannon round, one hit with a KEM is almost always enough to disable an enemy vehicle. The KEM is probably best used for conserving your "smart" missiles. Against targets like slow-flying transports, or Cruise missiles with a straight course, the KEM is devastating. Also, use it to knock out enemy aircraft on the ground. Save your Sidewinders and AMRAAMs for those enemy MiGs. For more information on KEMs, see earlier sections of this book.

Q: I've been winning most of my missions, but I was still pushed back into a previous sector. How can this happen?

A: As the saying goes, you can win all the battles and still lose the war. Actually, you probably chose missions with very low point values, and so you didn't accumulate enough points to progress. You can "cheat" by looking up the point value of a mission in this book before you fly it. The most valuable missions are worth 25 points.

Q: Why can't I destroy ground targets with the cannon or KEMs? I can hit aircraft on the ground, but not trucks or buildings.

A: This is simply the way the game is designed. The KEMs and the cannon are only good against aircraft (in flight and on the ground). The Sidewinder, AMRAAM, and Phoenix missiles will destroy buildings, trucks, and just about any ground target.

Q: I can't get [Alt][O], the Landscape Traversal Mode, to work all the time.

A: Landscape Traversal Mode is not available when you're flying missions in Adventure mode. If it were, that would make it too easy to disengage from the enemy during a dogfight, or to evade an enemy missile. Landscape Traversal Mode is available in all other flight modes: Free Flight, Instant Flight, and Combat Missions.

Q: I can't seem to choose the F-16 for missions!

A: The F-16 is not designed to take off from, or land on, an aircraft carrier. Because most missions in JetFighter II are carrier-based, the F-16 is not available as often as the other aircraft.

TECHNICAL QUESTIONS AND ANSWERS

This section discusses the most common technical, computer-related questions and problems encountered by JetFighter II users. If you have a problem running the game, or if something strange happens during the game, look here for the answer. If you have a question about game play, such as how to use the KEM missiles, see the "Game Play Questions and Answers" section, above.

Q: Everything was going fine, and now I'm in Sector 4, but some of the missions act really weird. Sometimes I fall through the carrier before I can even take off, and sometimes I'm coming in for a landing and the carrier deck disappears.

A: Some computers, in certain configurations, have had trouble with the Sector 4 mission data. Several missions in that sector may not function properly on your machine. A fix is available from Velocity. Or, if you have Compuserve, you can download the fix. GO GAMPUB and download JF2FIX1.ZIP from Library #16. Understand that this *does not* affect other parts of the game. This problem only occurred on the very first version of JetFighter II, and all the other missions should work fine. Don't send for the update unless you see this problem!

Q: JetFighter II used to work fine, but now I see a message that says "Packed File Corrupt."

A: You probably switched to DOS 5. There's a bug lurking around in one of the Microsoft programming utilities that we use. The problem is,you now have *too much* free memory. On some machines, when the program tries to load into the first 64K of memory, the "Packed File Corrupt" message may appear. DOS 5 users can solve the problem by using Microsoft's own fix: LOADFIX. Instead of typing **JF2** and pressing (Enter) to run JetFighter II, you should type **LOADFIX JF2** and press (Enter). If you don't have DOS 5, you'll have to use up some of your memory before running the game. Try launching a TSR program or increasing your files and buffers in the CONFIG.SYS file.

Q: I can't get JetFighter II to run under Microsoft Windows Version 3.0.

A: The very first release of JetFighter II is not compatible with Windows 3.0 in 386 enhanced mode. Both Windows and JetFighter are attempting to use privileged 386 features, and Windows won't let JetFighter II run. An update of JetFighter is available that should allow both programs to run. However, because JetFighter II is a very graphics-intensive program, it *will not* run in a window.

Q: I just installed DOS 5, and JetFighter won't run with the EMM386 expanded memory manger installed. The main menu works fine, but when I go to fly, the game locks up. *Or:* JetFighter won't run with QEMM installed. *Or:* JetFighter won't run with 386 To The Max installed. *Or:* I get the "Exception 13" error from QEMM. *Or:* I get an "EMM violation. . ." error from EMM386.

A: This is exactly like the Windows 3.0 problem above, and will occur only with the first version of JetFighter II. 386 expanded memory managers such as EMM386, QEMM, and 386MAX prevent other programs from using certain 386 features of your computer. JetFighter is trying to use these features and is "locked out" by the memory manager. To temporarily solve the problem, you can remove or "remark out" the memory manager from your CONFIG.SYS file. Consult your DOS manual for the way to do this. Alternatively, many users prefer to make a bootable DOS dist without a CONFIG.SYS file. This way you can boot up your computer with the DOS disk and run JetFighter from your hard drive without any problems. Also, Velocity has an update that solves this conflict with 386 memory managers. To get the update, return *one* of your original disk sets (either the *single* 5.25" *or* the *two* 3.5" disks) to Velocity with $4.00 to cover shipping and handling. They'll update your disks and send you the very latest version of JetFighter II.

Q: I get the message "Out of environment space" when running JetFighter II.

A: DOS sets aside some memory, called environment space. You need to increase the amount of this memory. This is done in your CONFIG.SYS file. You'll need to add a line to CONFIG.SYS that looks like this:

```
shell = c:\command.com /E:512
```

If you already have a line that looks like this, you need to add or increase the number after "/E:". The number after "/E:" is the number of bytes to be used for environment space. For example, if your line currently looks like this:

shell = c:\command.com /E:300

you should change it to:

shell = c:\command.com /E:512

This should allow JetFighter II to run without producing the "Out of environment space" error message.

Q: My joystick seems to be messing up. I can't get it to calibrate correctly.

A: Velocity has gone to great lengths to avoid any joystick incompatibility problems, but some combinations of joystick, game adapter, and computer still may cause trouble. I strongly suggest that you try to adjust your joystick adapter card. Many modern adapter cards have a switch setting that will help match the card to your computer. Try different settings on the card. You may find that one setting works *much* better than the others.

Q: I started a new pilot, and suddenly all my joystick settings are gone.

A: Each pilot in the roster has his own unique joystick settings. This is because most players like to customize the settings to their particular flying styles. When you start a new pilot, you'll have to calibrate the joystick before it can be used. Don't forget to save the settings before you quit!

Q: I installed the game on the hard disk, but when I run it, it says "Please Insert the Mission Disk in drive C:".

A: Something went wrong with the installation. Either your hard disk didn't have enough free space, or you didn't follow the installation instructions. You may have typed **a:install** and pressed [Enter], instead of typing **a:**, pressing [Enter], typing **install**, and pressing [Enter]. Installation must be done in two steps, as described in the manual. First delete any JetFighter II files on your hard disk. Next, check to make sure that you have at least 1 megabyte of free space on your hard disk. Now reinstall JetFighter II, following the directions exactly as they appear in the manual.

Q: I have a VGA card. The Main menu and startup screens appear correctly, but when I go to fly, the display is screwy. I see garbage that almost looks like many little cockpits on the screen.

A: You probably have a software-compatible-only VGA card, such as the ATI VIP VGA card. These older VGA cards are not 100 percent VGA-compatible, and will not run much of today's modern VGA software. In order to run in VGA mode, you *must* have a 100 percent hardware-compatible VGA card. 99.99 percent of all VGA cards made in the last several years are hardware-compatible with the VGA. If you have an older (and incompatible) board, you may want to consider upgrading. These days, basic VGA boards can be found for as little as $60.

Q: I get the music from my MicroChannel AdLib board, but I can't get any sound effects during the game.

A: This is a strange problem with MicroChannel AdLib boards that Velocity is trying to solve. You'll need to check in with Velocity to see if an update is available yet.

Q: Will a math coprocessor chip speed up the performance of JetFighter II?

A: No, it won't. Velocity already uses optimized integer math, which is far faster than math done with the coprocessor. If you need better performance, consider upgrading your machine or adding an accelerator card.

Q: I have a Super-VGA card. Why does JetFighter II still run in low-resolution graphics mode?

A: Higher-resolution graphics modes are too slow to provide the fast frame rate that JetFighter is known for. 640 x 480 x 256-color mode requires *five times* as much processor time to draw to the screen. Even on a super-fast PC, JetFighter II would probably be too slow to be any fun. Hopefully the industry will begin to produce practical graphics coprocessor accelerator cards, which will let Velocity improve the resolution and the colors.

Q: Can I run JetFighter II from a RAM disk?

A: Sure, but it won't improve the frame rate, because JetFighter II actually does very little disk access while flying. However, you will notice faster game loading times. If you're playing the Adventure section of JetFighter II, don't forget to copy your ROSTER.DAT file back to the hard disk before you turn off your computer.

Q: I'm buying a new computer. What's the best computer I can get to make JetFighter run as fast as possible?

A: Get the fastest computer you can afford. A 386-33 or 486 will make JetFighter II look great. A fast 16-bit VGA board will help too. Don't worry about math coprocessors (see question above).

Q: I'll be flying along in a mission without any problems, then all of a sudden I'm flying into a building and there's a big explosion. Then the mission ends.

A: That's not you that flew into the building—it was an enemy Cruise missile. In some missions the enemy can actually win. If you take too long to complete such missions, you'll be presented with a scene of the enemy's missile hitting its target. By the way, you can use all the normal exterior view controls to look at the missile before it hits!

Q: I never really get a good look at the enemy. In all my other simulators, I can stay right on his tail and keep him in my sights the whole time.

A: Most other simulators greatly exaggerate the size of enemy aircraft. In other words, an enemy MiG may appear 4 to 8 times its actual size. They do this so you *can* get a good look at him. In JetFighter the aircraft's size is not exaggerated. Velocity wants you to see just how hard it is to tell friend from foe. Not to mention that it's pretty hard to stay right on someone's tail at 1400 miles per hour.

Q: I read that the Phoenix missiles on the F-14 have a 100-mile range. Why don't I get target lock-on at 100 miles in my F-14?

A: The answer is simple. Velocity didn't think it would be much fun to kill the enemy without ever getting into a dogfight. They do make tradeoffs when designing their products, and the 100-mile range of the Phoenix was one of them. They think it makes for much better game play.

Q: I've tried everything, but JetFighter II just won't run. Sometimes the Main menu will work OK, but the flight portion won't load.

A: You may have a "mixed" or "impure" version of DOS on your machine. The part of DOS that runs your application consists primarily of three files. You may be familiar with one of these, COMMAND.COM. The other two are hidden files that DOS installs on your disk. If all three files are not from the *same version* and *same brand* of DOS, JetFighter II (and some other programs) may not run properly. You can check this as follows: Type **ver** and press Enter, and note the brand and version of DOS. Now, type **command** and press Enter, and note the brand and version of DOS. If these don't match, you need to update DOS on your disk. You can do this with the SYS command. See your DOS manual, or your dealer, for more information.

Q: What is the best way to contact Velocity?

A: The absolute best way to contact Velocity is through electronic mail (e-mail). Velocity regularly visits forums on Compuserve and Prodigy. If you like, you can send private mail to their addresses as follows:

> CompuServe   76670,2202
>
> Prodigy   VFSS19A

Or write to:

> Velocity Development
> P.O. Box 875
> Palatine, IL 60078-0875

Q: I use Norton's Speed Disk. It says most of the JetFighter files are "unmovable."

A: I don't know why Norton does this, but there's no problem with moving the JetFighter files. Simply remove them from Norton's "unmovable file" list and compress your disk as usual. You may want to save this setting to disk for the future.use.

Q: The colors on my game seem bad. I can't see the cockpit details and the carrier at night is almost invisible.

A: Try adjusting the contrast and brightness on your monitor. Velocity uses very subtle shades of grey that may not appear correctly if your monitor adjustments are wrong. Most other programs you use probably don't show as many colors as JetFighter II.

Q: The keyboard controls don't seem to be working very well. They've become sluggish.

A: If you typically use both the keyboard *and* the joystick, you may need to adjust your joystick settings. If your joystick doesn't return to center properly after you release it, JetFighter may think you're still trying to fly with the joystick. Because of this, the keyboard will not be "scanned" as often. This can cause the "sluggishness" you're getting. There are two solutions. First, if you turn the joystick *off* using the JetFighter inflight menu, the keyboard should respond correctly again. However, simply increasing the Dead Zone setting a little bit will make the program recognize that your joystick has returned to center. For example, if the Dead Zone is at 8, increase it to 12 and see if that helps.

Q: I couldn't find the serial number on my JetFighter II disks. Will you still register me?

A: Of course. Some serial numbers were placed on the back of the 5.25" disks and were hard to find. Don't worry—the serial number is not as important as filling out your registration card and sending it to Velocity. Hey, they trust you!

Q: Does JetFighter II have a "demo" mode?

A: No. There's no built-in demo with JetFighter II. There is, however, a separate stand-alone demo, which is available for downloading on Compuserve and may even be at your local software store. (This demo is a great way to show off your computer!)

Q: All I ever get is NO TARG in my air targets display.

A: Before you can track an enemy aircraft, you have to target it. This is done with the T key. Pressing T will cycle through every target that is within your current radar range. If there are no blips on your radar, there are no targets to select.

Q: Does Velocity have a multi-player or network version available?

A: Not yet. This is something Velocity would really like to do, but they won't promise any dates.

Q: Does JetFighter II support rudder pedals or a second joystick for yaw and throttle?

A: As of now, JetFighter II only supports a single joystick.

Q: My JetFighter II box came with two 3.5" disks and only one 5.25" disk. Is this right? Shouldn't I have more 5.25" disks?

A: No! That is a *high-density* 5.25" disk. It contains all the files that are on the two 3.5" disks. Velocity simply dual-packs the game as a convenience to users.

Q: How do I make a backup of my pilot's information? I don't want to lose my progress if I have a hard disk crash.

A: The information for all of the pilots in the roster is stored in a file called ROSTER.DAT. If you're familiar with DOS, make a backup of this file as needed.

Q: My mouse doesn't seem to work with the game.

A: First, understand that you can't use the mouse to fly the aircraft. It's only active during the Main Menu section of the game. If the mouse pointer acts strange, doesn't appear, or leaves "garbage" on the screen, you probably need to get an updated *mouse driver* from the company that made your mouse. Your mouse and mouse driver must be 100 percent Microsoft-compatible.

Q: JetFighter II seems to be messing up my system clock.

A: On certain computers, the first release of JetFighter II may have caused the clock to lose time. This has been solved, and an update is available from Velocity. Write or call for more information.

Q: The pilot record is not keeping correct count of my day and night carrier traps.

A: Under some circumstances, these statistics were not recorded correctly in the very first release of JetFighter II. If you notice this problem and would like an update, write or call Velocity.

Q: The mission orders say I should be taking off from one location, but I actually start from a different location.

A: This problem occurred on some machines with the very first release of JetFighter II. It does not affect the game in any other way. If you need an update, write or call Velocity.

Q: Sometimes when I release a bomb, instead of hitting the ground it jumps up to 20,000 feet and takes forever to fall.

A: This is a strange problem with the very first release of JetFighter II. It only happens with bombs #3 and #4 of a 12-bomb load on the ATF. An update is available; write or call for details.

Index

NOW AVAILABLE

COMPUTER GAME BOOKS

SimEarth: The Official Strategy Guide	$18.95
Harpoon Battlebook	$18.95
Wing Commander I and II: The Ultimate Strategy Guide	$18.95
Chuck Yeager's Air Combat Handbook	$18.95
The Official Lucasfilm Games Air Combat Strategies Book	$18.95
Sid Meier's Civilization, or Rome on 640K a Day	$18.95
Ultima: The Avatar Adventures	$18.95
JetFighter II: The Official Strategy Guide	$18.95
A-Train: The Official Strategy Guide	$18.95
PowerMonger: The Official Strategy Guide	$18.95
Global Conquest: The Official Strategy Guide (w/disk)	$24.95
Heaven & Earth: The Official Strategy Guide	$18.95
Falcon 3: The Official Combat Strategy Book (w/disk)	$27.95
Dynamix Great War Planes: The Ultimate Strategy Guide	$18.95

COMING SOON

COMPUTER GAME BOOKS

Lemmings: The Official Companion (w/disk)	$24.95	(Dec.)
V for Victory: The Official Battleplan for Normandy	$18.95	(Jan.)
Gunship 2000: The Authorized Strategy Guide	$18.95	(Jan.)
LucasArts Adventure Book	$18.95	(Jan.)
Stunt Island: The Official Strategy Guide	$18.95	(Jan.)
Populous I and II: The Official Strategy Guide	$18.95	(Jan.)

NOW AVAILABLE

VIDEO GAME BOOKS

Nintendo Games Secrets, Volumes 1, 2, 3, and 4	$9.99	each
Nintendo Game Boy Secrets, Volumes 1 and 2	$9.99	each
Sega Genesis Secrets, Volumes 1, 2, and 3	$9.99	each
Official Sega Genesis Power Tips Book (in full color!)	$14.99	
TurboGrafx-16 and TurboExpress Secrets, Volumes 1 and 2	$9.99	each
Super NES Games Secrets, Volumes 1, 2, and 3	$9.99	each
GamePro Presents: Nintendo Games Secrets Greatest Tips	$9.99	
GamePro Presents: Sega Genesis Games Secrets Greatest Tips	$9.99	
Super Mario World Games Secrets	$12.99	
The Legend of Zelda: A Link to the Past Game Secrets	$12.99	

COMING SOON

VIDEO GAME BOOKS

Sega Genesis Secrets, Volume 4	$9.99	(Jan.)

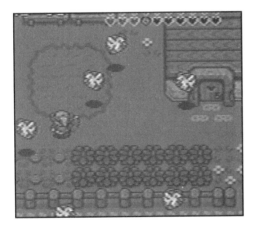

TO ORDER BOOKS

Please send me the following items:

Quantity	Title	Unit Price	Total
_____	_____	$_____	$_____
_____	_____	$_____	$_____
_____	_____	$_____	$_____
_____	_____	$_____	$_____
_____	_____	$_____	$_____
_____	_____	$_____	$_____
	Subtotal		$_____
	7.25% SALES TAX (CALIFORNIA ONLY)		$_____
	SHIPPING		$ __3.99__
	TOTAL ORDER		$_____

By telephone: With Visa or MC, call (916) 786-0426.
Mon.–Fri. 9–4 PST. By mail: Just fill out the
information below and send with your remittance to:

PRIMA PUBLISHING
P.O. Box 1260BK
Rocklin, CA 95677

Satisfaction unconditionally guaranteed

My name is_____

I live at_____

City_____ State_____ Zip_____

Visa / MC#_____Exp._____

Signature_____